Praise for Boardroom to Base Camp

"Boardroom to Base Camp is not just another business book. Todd Millar's Everest Model is a primer for life and leadership, whether leading a company, a family or finding your own quality of life. It is part spiritual awakening and part swift kick in the butt; a reality check about who you are, and more importantly, how you inspire others."

- **Mikki Williams**, CSP
Multi-preneur, Professional Speaker,
Vistage Chair and *Mensch*

"Within 24 hours of reading Boardroom to Base Camp, I found myself reciting Todd Millar's wisdom. You will assimilate these life lessons into your own personal journey by the time you finish this fabulous story. Now I feel like I've known Todd for my whole life, and I have a great deal of admiration for his journey and application of the Everest Model."

- **W.B. (Liam) Christie**
Chair, Prairies & TEC305,
TEC Canada

"Todd Millar's account of his ascent to Mount Everest Base Camp, and its parallel to the business world, is remarkable. The development of a strong Foundation in Todd's Everest Model, as well as the development of a Vision when it can be difficult to see what the ultimate goal is, resonated with me. This method has already helped me focus my approach to work with clients and colleagues.

- **Ian H. Gunn,** CA, CMA
PricewaterhouseCoopers LLP
Partner, Audit and Assurance Group

"What a great story! But, more importantly, what a wonderful way to find our place in the world, truly feel like we belong, and that we can make a difference in making the world a better place. Boardroom to Base Camp is packed with thought-provoking exercises and simple, yet powerful principles to live by, as we make our way through life at home and at work."

- **James W. Kraemer,** FCA, CFP, TEP
TFI Financial Services,
FundEX Investments Inc.

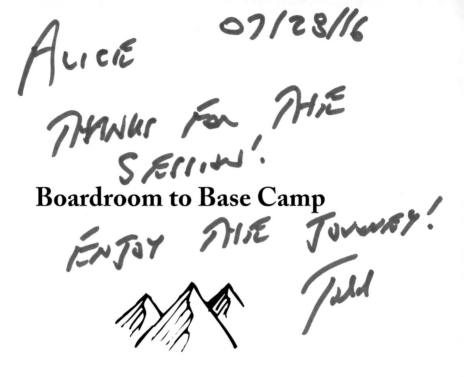

ALICE
07/28/16

THANKS FOR THE
SESSION!

ENJOY THE JOURNEY!

Todd

Boardroom to Base Camp

Life and Leadership Lessons from the Top

From the 2.6 Billion Dollar Sale of SuperPages
to Base Camp of Mount Everest

BOARDROOM TO BASE CAMP
Life and Leadership Lessons from the Top

Copyright © 2013 Todd Millar, *www.toddmillarspeaking.com*

Published by:
Blooming Twig Books
New York / Tulsa
www.bloomingtwig.com

Front cover design by LPI Group, *www.lpi-group.com*
Front cover photograph of Mount Everest taken by
Byron Smith from the top of Kala Patthar (5,550 m).

Hardcover: ISBN 978-1-61343-36-1
Paperback: ISBN 978-1-61343-017-0
eBook: ISBN 978-1-61343-027-9

First Edition
Printed in Canada

To all the great contributors in my life.

There are so many. I have been very fortunate to
have worked with some of the best, had friends of
great influence, have been reminded of the basic
essentials in life, have been kept grounded
by my family, and loved by all.

Boardroom to Base Camp

Life and Leadership Lessons from the Top

From the 2.6 Billion Dollar Sale of SuperPages
to Base Camp of Mount Everest

Blooming Twig Books
New York / Tulsa

Table of Contents

Foreword

by Zeke O'Connor
Founder & Past-President of the
Sir Edmund Hillary Foundation,
Author of *Journey with the Sherpas*

One of my closest business associates was the late Sir Edmund Hillary, the first man to summit Mount Everest. I spent much of my time in both business and charity work by his side – we co-founded the Sir Edmund Hillary Foundation, and worked together to help the Sherpa people of Nepal. Over 35 years, I observed Sir Edmund, who was already a bona fide leader, explorer, and sincere humanitarian, develop into a tremendously successful philanthropic figure.

Over time, I have enjoyed the benefits of a close association with many other very successful individuals as well: business leaders, sports figures, humanitarians and international political leaders. I consider Todd Millar one of these special individuals for his achievements in the worlds of both business and hockey, for helping young people achieve their goals, and because he consciously lives an exemplary family life. I am also pleased to announce that Todd was recently elected as a director on the Sir Edmund Hillary Foundation Board of Directors, and in his new role, Todd will play an important part in helping the foundation assist the Sherpa people of the Mount Everest area.

I have known Todd Millar for almost three years. We met through our mutual friend Byron Smith, a well-known mountaineer, who led Todd's group on their trek to Base Camp – a life changing experience that greatly impacted Todd's thinking. In fact, on the pages of *Boardroom to Base Camp,* I notice remarkable similarities between Sir Edmund's and Todd's detailed approaches to success.

I was in the village of Phaflu, Nepal, the day Todd and his son T.J. arrived, and I had a chance to speak with them there. I spoke with them again during their ascent at the Kunde Hospital just below Base Camp (13,700 feet), and at that point, T.J. and Todd were looking forward to getting started on the most difficult part of their journey. I could see that they worked well together and had trained hard in preparation to meet the physiological and psychological challenges ahead. They had built a strong foundation for their journey.

I have faced many challenges over more than 80 years on this Earth, and without a strong foundation, I don't know what I might have achieved. My childhood in a large family during the Great Depression became the personal foundation upon which I built most everything I sought to accomplish.

In the pages that follow, Todd Millar uses his Everest Model to help each reader solidify his or her solid foundation, upon which all successes can thereafter be built. From there, Todd inspires all of us to reach far beyond our immediate goals.

Good reading and enjoy the journey!

Namaste,

Zeke O'Connor

Preface

"It's Never Enough"

We were on top of the world. Bain Capital had just brokered a deal for the sale of SuperPages Canada (the company of which I was president) for $2.6 billion dollars, making a record-breaking profit of $700 million dollars in the span of one year. We were also *literally* on top of the world, or so it felt. Our celebration was taking place at an unbelievable restaurant in Boston.

I had first gotten into telecommunications in the 1990's after many years in different sectors, and had worked my way up through the ranks of the Canadian division of Verizon Information Services – eventually taking on the role of company president. Under my leadership, we sold the company to Bain Capital in 2004 for a "cool" $1.9 billion dollars.

At that point, some of the leadership at Bain invited me to their headquarters in Boston, where we met over dinner, and I was asked to continue my role as President within the company – I would be working for them. I agreed, and was thrilled to build a new executive team and get started.

Before this pivotal moment in my career, I had already spent time in countless boardrooms. I was blessed with early success in my climb up the corporate ladder, working with such great companies as Canadian Tire (in the Petroleum Division), Turbo Resources (which was eventually taken over by Shell), and Telus. At the time, I had no vision of what was evolving in my career, or that I would reach the height of a $2.6 billion dollar sale under Bain Capital. However, all of my experiences at these companies in various senior capacities contributed to the development of the Everest Model that I have now lain out between these covers.

My time at Bain was absolutely incredible. I felt a huge sense of freedom – this was a different world than the boardroom I had always known. Then, as a result of seven months of hard work, Bain Capital was able to sell SuperPages Canada to a competitor for $2.6 billion dollars. We were over the moon.

At the champagne dinner and celebration in Boston, I shook many hands and slapped a lot of backs. It was incredible for someone in my early 40's – it was a time of real awakening for me. I will always be extremely thankful for the opportunity that Bain Capital provided to my executive team and me. Their leadership and approach to our business, entrusting the operations to the "operators" created the right environment for a great story to be told.

The party was kind of a who's who of the financial markets. All of those who were involved with this incredible transaction were there. It was a very special evening celebration, given the incredible accomplishment by so many in such a short period of time. In less than a year, SuperPages Canada had made Bain Capital $700 million dollars.

At that party, a very influential businessman came over to me and shook my hand, and he said a few words that would change the rest of my life. He came up to me, shook my hand, and then said with a truthful smile, "You know something, Todd? It's never enough."

This businessman knew that I was walking away from this transaction with a sizable sum of money. It was more than I had ever earned in my career by any standard. And he knew what presumably usually happened to people like me: I would never feel like I had enough. I would continue to pursue wealth, and devote my entire life to that one purpose.

Those words and that experience were incredibly profound to me. For the next several years, I often let my mind wander and think, "What's next in life? If it's never enough, do I have to go and do other things? Do I have to go run another company? Will $10 million dollars be enough? How about $100 million?

The reality is, immediately following the transaction, I began feeling a sense of loss. I couldn't answer the question, "What's next?" Whether that feeling came over me as the result of the temptation that was explained by the Boston businessman's statement, "It's never enough," or from other circumstances in my life at the time, I felt this sense of loss for several years. At the same time, I was blessed to be able to spend more time with my family, and even share a journey with my son to Mount Everest Base Camp. On that journey, I finally found the transformation I was seeking, and began to realize what was next. I came to the realization that we had more than enough.

This concept of "more than enough" clearly varies from person to person, but is the true definition of *abundance*. When we dig a little deeper, most of us will discover that what we *have* is already more than enough. It is simply the *choices* we make that create the belief within us that "it is never enough."

In October 2010, I first learned about the Sir Edmund Hillary Foundation when a friend invited us to a benefit dinner. Sir Edmund Hillary had been the first man to successfully summit Everest, and with his business partner Zeke O'Connor, established this foundation primarily to raise money for schools and medical centers in the Himalayan Mountains of Nepal for the Sherpa people who live there.

That night, Barbra can confirm that I had a glass of wine or two, whereupon I proceeded to bid on an item that would again bring me to the top of the world (or close to it). I raised my hand at the auction when a trip for two came on the block. My wife looked at me like I was crazy, and I think I probably was. I was the successful bidder on a trip for two to Mount Everest Base Camp.

On the way home, Barbra and I already began debating about this crazy acquisition of mine, and what we could do with the trip. I had been refereeing hundreds of hockey games every year, and I was in very good physical shape (or so I thought), and I hoped that someone would take this adventure with me. My first thought was to go with Barbra, but she had just undergone reconstructive knee surgery, so that wouldn't work. Then we thought about my daughter, Larissa, but she is a Type I diabetic, which, we thought, could end up being a nightmare up on Mount Everest. My son, T.J., was in 11th grade at the time, but he was very mature, and we thought that this could be an incredible, life-altering experience for him. It was settled: it would be a father and son trip. We arrived home late that night and couldn't wait to share the news and discover his interest. He was very excited, to say the least.

My son and I trained together for the trip. Actually, my son was 16 and an elite-level hockey player who didn't require much training, and let's just say that I probably should have trained a little more! T.J. and I then traveled to Nepal to start our journey to Mount Everest Base Camp, where you can see the world stretch out before you. It was an incredible moment for a father and a son, and it was something I could never have "afforded" to do if I had inherited the mentality of the Boston businessman who said I would never have enough. Indeed, I had *more* than I would ever have had while still in the corporate world.

This book is what has come out of my thought process around my experience in boardrooms, from the bottom of the corporate ladder to a place near the top, and my experience with my son on the tallest mountain in the world. I never would have thought there would be so many similarities – I certainly wasn't trekking to Base Camp of Everest and thinking about the corporate ladder. But in hindsight, I saw how being "on top of the world" has its benefits and its drawbacks. From there, I thought about every stage of the journey, and I thought of the traits one needs to achieve success – whether climbing a mountain or doing your job well.

While looking at photos of my trip to Everest with my son, I began to envision the Everest Model that you will see in these pages. Our lives are incredibly busy today – I've attempted to make the Everest Model as simple as possible to integrate into your daily life. My humble suggestion is that you read this book slowly, and write in it as you would a journal. Think of the book as your guide on Mount Everest (few people attempt to climb Everest without a guide!). Whether you are climbing the corporate ladder, or working on a personal objective, the three Rules, the five Principles, and 15 Ingredients (three per Principle) of this Everest Model with disciplined application will drive your continuing success, both at home and at work.

The limits are only defined by your ambition, drive and determination. It is my belief that by adhering to the Everest Model and the simple applications of the model, you will be equipping yourself with all of the "right stuff" to support yourself in your own journey of success.

Our individual choice and *ability* to choose is the real power – and we all possess that power. Whether we are climbing a mountain or crouched in a cubicle, we are all on a similar journey.

Enjoy the climb!

- R. Todd Millar, November 2012

Introduction

An Incredible Moment in Time

I proudly wear many hats in my life: among other things, I am a father of two wonderful kids, a husband, a hockey referee, a professional speaker, and an executive coach. However, when I speak to groups of every size, or do one-on-one training with leaders, they all ask me to tell them about the biggest moment of my business career: the sale of SuperPages Canada that made Bain Capital $700 million dollars within seven months, going from a purchase of $1.9 billion dollars to a sale of $2.6 billion dollars.

In order to properly set the scene, I will start at the end of the story. At a farewell dinner in Banff, Alberta, I gathered with my outgoing executive team for a celebration, and, in essence, a goodbye. I had been their President for the last several months, at Advertising Directory Solutions (ADS), otherwise known as SuperPages Canada, and we had just successfully sold the company – an incredible, yet bittersweet, moment in all of our lives. We were sitting in the conference room of the Rimrock Resort Hotel in Banff National Park, perched on the side of a mountain, looking out the wall-to-floor windows at the snowcapped and rugged 10,000-foot peaks of the Canadian Rocky Mountains, humbled by our surroundings, and amazed by our recent success. That day, I handed out a small clock to each member of my team with the inscription: "An Incredible Moment in Time," along with their name and the date. It was a small memento, especially compared to the size of the cheques they had just received a few days before, but it was a reminder of our incredible journey together.

I wasn't some guy that was born with a silver spoon in his mouth. I also didn't graduate with my MBA and suddenly find myself launched into the role of Vice President. This is the part of my story that I enjoy telling people *more* than the part about the victory party in Banff, because it's a story that so many of us share.

I started this portion of my career with Telus, a telecommunication company, in 1994. I began running what they called "Electronic Information Services", and I became in charge of our handheld PDA devices, which were leading technology at that time. Those devices ran on PCMCI technology, and contained one- and two-megabyte memory cards.

This was the highest technology on the market, and it was really exciting to be part of the sales team there, and the aggressive plan to grow across Canada.

My next step was one I questioned in many ways at first. I got a job as a Regional Sales Manager for Yellow Pages. Quite frankly, it didn't excite me that much, and I thought, *Really, is this going to be my career? Selling the Yellow Pages?* Nevertheless, I took that job for two reasons. First, I thought it was time for someone else to step in – I had launched this handheld PDA device across the real estate industry, and I thought someone else had to take it to the next level. And second, and most important, that job had me on the road from Monday through Friday all across Canada, opening up new markets on behalf of Telus, and I wasn't able to get enough face time with my young family.

A job that I thought would be boring quickly turned into an opportunity for me. I began to see how the company could change and improve, and I soon found myself invigorated, and was promoted to the level of Vice President of Sales. Ironically, this had been my choice of a job that would allow me to spend more time with my family and travel less, but ended up being a job where I was home even less than I had been with the previous job. Yellow Pages was sold to Verizon, and the company would no longer be just an Alberta company – they would be a company that would span from coast to coast in Canada. Here I was again, airplane-hopping around Canada and setting up competitive markets on the East Coast, in Halifax, and all the way across to Vancouver. In the following chapters, I will cover my later decisions that led to more time with my family and the creation of the Everest Model that is the core of this book. But it's important that I first describe the series of events that propelled me quickly forward in my career.

Over the next eight years, during my time as the Vice President of Sales for Yellow Pages, nothing stayed the same. There were four major leadership changes in that amount of time, so I got to be a part of an incredible amount of shakeup and change. I began to see a cycle develop, and I called it the *three-year agony*. The first year, a new leader would come in and bump around, kind of looking at things. The second year, the leader will make a bunch of changes, some of them sweeping. And, without fail, around the third year, the leader would leave, because that was when they realized all of the changes they had enacted had been ineffective or just plain wrong. Ever since then, I define a great, successful executive as somebody who can stay on beyond those three years. Long story short, four different leaders cycled through our company during those eight years, and none of them outlasted the *three-year agony*.

The only thing to which I could compare our eight years of uncertainty at Yellow Pages would be foster care. As adoptive parents of two amazing children, Barbra and I have heard many stories about foster care, and how kids are often tossed from family to family, and uncertainty becomes a permanent fixture in their lives. I was part of what seemed like a foster-child-company, bounced around from owner to owner, changing leadership, changing names, and changing everything else but a few core elements. I was part of that core, and stayed with the company through this difficult time, but it was not easy.

After eight years, the President of Verizon Information Services (our new parent company), Kathy Harless, who was located in Dallas, Texas at the time, announced to us that SuperPages Canada was for sale. I was asked to take the lead role in the sale of the company – something that seemed like a strange request at the time. I was the Vice President of Sales, but I had never sold anything like a multi-million dollar company, and I didn't even know where to begin. I was informed that the process was to be a "bidding process," and I was so green when it came to this kind of transaction, that I thought a person or organization would purchase our company in a big auction.

The bidding process was not as related to eBay as I had first thought, and I quickly learned the ropes, and did the best I could to orient myself to the business of large transactions. The targets would be private equity firms like KKR, Carlyle Group and Bain Capital. In all, we prepared for, and then gave twelve presentations, each four hours in length, led by a small group of executives from my company. I was at the helm of those presentations, and we worked hard on building a marketing pitch that would interest our suitors. At the end of a grueling month, there were only three companies left, and three sealed bids were delivered to Verizon head-quarters. Bain Capital had the winning bid, and they purchased SuperPages Canada for a cool $1.9 billion dollars.

My job was over. I had successfully completed the mission and believed my next journey would begin with a new career.

I will never forget the phone call I received asking me to attend a dinner in Boston with Bain Capital. When I arrived in Boston, I was a pretty exhausted guy. I had been through the wringer, and I was satisfied with the work we had done, and where we had ended up. This was the end of the road for this particular part of my life and career. Or so I thought …

In Boston, as I sat with the executives at Bain Capital, I quickly figured out that they were sizing me up to see whether I would be willing to lead the company under their new ownership. They told me, "We've heard great things about you," and I started to buy into what they were saying. These guys were pouring the metaphorical Kool-Aid on the table in front of me, and I was going to drink it. There was no monkey-business here; they talked to me straight from the hip. They told me it would be a five-year play in typical private equity fashion. Five to seven years, maximum, and they wanted to be out with their money. They asked me, "Will you be the guy to take us there?" Apparently, my presentation to them the previous month had struck a chord, and they asked if I would continue on with them in the role of President of SuperPages Canada.

That Boston dinner was where my admiration for Bain's style began. Six business people met with me – a Canadian executive who knew little to nothing about their world. Yet they created a relaxing environment where hierarchy was blurred; I even remember having to ask who reported to whom. They chuckled as if that was the furthest thing of importance in their world. Clearly this was going to be like nothing I had ever experienced.

That evening, the Bain executives excitedly told me their entire game plan. They laid out the strategy at a high level, and they expressed confidence in my ability to select the right team and implement certain improvements that would result in profits over five to seven years. This was pretty exciting stuff for a guy who was on the verge of burnout. Before that night, I had just wanted to get the heck out of this business, and try my hand at another job – I was 41 years old and had other opportunities in mind. I was caught off guard; this was an exciting opportunity that I couldn't pass up. I accepted the role and the challenge, and I started off on the journey of a lifetime.

I flew back home, kissed my wife, looked at my kids and said, "Hey, this is going to be an exciting opportunity! Your daddy's a new President!"

Shortly after that dinner meeting I reported back to Boston. For the next several weeks I would either be in Boston or New York as we prepared for what they called the *Roadshow*. Bain was injecting $500 million dollars into SuperPages Canada right away, and would get loans for the rest. I didn't understand at the time exactly what that meant, but I soon found out that my team would have to raise the other $1.4 billion dollars in capital. At this point in my life, I had barely seen $10,000 dollars at a time in our bank account, and all of a sudden I was in charge of raising $1.4 billion dollars. How on earth would this work?

I found myself in New York City with a room full of bankers, and I was completely overwhelmed. They talked about a $700 million dollar coupon here, a $250 million dollar coupon there, and I started to think to myself, *Do you understand that I'm not that smart? I've never done this!*

When I am describing this process to people, I usually talk about something that just about all of us have had experience with: buying a house. Let's say that you are buying a $1.9 billion dollar house. Your down-payment for that transaction is $500 million dollars. That's all the money you can possible spend – you scraped it together from all of your friends and family, but you just can't find any more. You will have to go talk to various banks to try to take out a mortgage on the balance. Guess what? Banks don't go around giving $1.4 billion dollar mortgages, so you actually have to get three different types of mortgages: one will be a line of credit, another will be a high-interest loan, and the third will be a long-term mortgage.

In this case, Bain Capital intended to purchase the "house" in order to flip it, or sell it for a profit. So, their goal was to pay the debt, secure mortgages for $1.4 billion dollars, and then sell it within five to seven years at a profit. They intended to fix up the house, clean it up, put paint on the walls, knock down a few walls, do some gardening, and so forth – but that would take five to seven years. At that point, if market conditions went well, they could put a big for sale sign up and someone would buy it for more than $1.9 billion dollars. They would pay off the $1.4 billion dollars in loans, get their $500 million dollars back out, and then get an extra $250 million or so in profit. Boy, that was a lot of hard work, but they will have made a good amount of money at the end of those five to seven years. Bain Capital's team explained this entire world of private equity to me, and they put a lot of confidence in me. That helped me to realize that it *would* be possible. I trusted in their confidence, because I had very little of my own.

Before the Roadshow began, I had tenuous belief, at best, in my team's ability to raise $1.4 billion dollars. I vividly remember waking up in New York City one particular morning, looking out over Central

Park with this feeling of, *Oh my goodness, I'm in over my head. How am I going to present this? How will I ever be successful at what these guys are asking me to do?*

I shrugged off my doubts, and headed to our meeting with a few hundred bankers that would hopefully result in a raise of $250 million dollars. This was our very first presentation, kick-starting the Roadshow, and alongside the hundreds of bankers gathered in their expensive suits to hear our presentation, the Bain Capital executives and all major employees of the company were there. All of them would be given the opportunity to invest some of their hard-earned money into this new private equity play.

Despite my fears, our presentations were extremely well received, and there was palpable excitement in the room. We had rehearsed and carefully planned this event, and we couldn't have hoped for a better result. People told me that they absolutely *believed* where this company was headed, and what it would be able to do. As a result, Bain was over-subscribed on that first coupon, before we put any miles on the Roadshow. And every single Bain Capital employee present that day agreed to participate – something that had never happened in the history of the company.

Over the course of the next ten days, our Roadshow team, led by me and my newfound colleague Mark Verdi as CFO, prepared for two weeks to present 46 times in 38 cities – all towards the goal of raising the cash to close this deal. It was intense, to say the least. I have never been an actor or in theatre, but I would liken those rehearsals to what preparations for a Broadway musical must be like. Every slide, statement and potential question was rehearsed.

The Red Sox were playing the New York Yankees in the 2004 World Series at the time, which added to the excitement and tension in the room (since we were in Boston). We were inspired by the Red Sox's victory, and we took that inspiration with us over the following weeks.

The first time I realized we might be going to the metaphorical playoffs was when I was sitting next to Mark in a limousine in San Francisco. He told me, halfway through our planned Roadshow, that we had already raised $1.4 billion dollars in subscriptions. I had some idea of what that meant, but I asked him to explain. He said to me, "Todd, you don't have any clue about what I'm talking about, do you?"

I said, "You're right, Mark. Tell me what's going on." I could tell this was great news from the look on his face, but I needed to know more.

He said, "We're already over-subscribed."

I had little knowledge of what being "over-subscribed" would mean, so I asked, "Does that mean we're done?"

Mark laughed and said, "No, we're going to keep going. We're going to see how many more subscriptions we can get."

We had reached our goal, and we had half of the presentations left to give! We ended up being three times oversubscribed by the end of the Roadshow – which eventually drove down the subscription rates – which I would liken to winning the World Series. For the Red Sox, the "curse of the Bambino" had been lifted, and for me, after nearly a decade of working with a company that was in turmoil and change all the time, we had won a great victory.

The next phase was (back to the house analogy) renovation. We were planning on repairing and re-building the company, so that it would be profitable within the next five to seven years. Months went by and we enjoyed the fruits of our efforts. Although we were headed into the cold of a Canadian winter, we felt fresh and alive and full of optimism about our future. But the future was about to change dramatically.

I remember the day that one of the senior executives at Bain called and nonchalantly mentioned in the course of the conversation that the CEO of Yellow Pages Group in Montreal was interested in buying SuperPages. We both chuckled at the notion, because we thought, *The company was just bought for a substantial amount of money. Who could really afford to buy us at more than $1.9 billion dollars?* We basically blew it off, not thinking that it would go through.

Weeks went by and we carried on, highly focused on our mission. It didn't occur to us that negotiations were happening behind closed doors. Soon, however, executives talked with me and made it clear that discussions with the Yellow Pages Group had become serious. And, suddenly, within a seven-day window, Yellow Pages Group put an offer of $2.6 billion dollars on the table.

On a Saturday evening, I was asked to participate in a conference call – something that we often did when Bain had official company business to discuss. I was downstairs in my home, sitting in my office. I dialed into a conference call where the members of the company board were then informed of talks that were going on, and that those negotiations had reached a critical point and the company could be sold for $2.6 billion dollars, subject to some due diligence. As we went around the virtual table on the phone call, I remember one of the principals asking me the question, "Todd what are your thoughts?"

I was honored that he had requested my opinion, and I said, "You know, where business is concerned, everything in life is for sale. That's the most important thing we've got to remember." This sale would mean a $700 million dollar profit for Bain Capital within several months. There weren't too many people scratching their heads around this deal. The sale transpired, and the $2.6 billion dollar acquisition was realized.

At the end of the conference call, I was asked to stay on the line. Members of the Bain team shared with me their great pride and gratitude for what my team had accomplished. I was beaming with excitement as I heard the accolades. Bain was also so pleased, they would pay out *all* expected performance bonuses, had my team served the years it would have taken to take the company public or to a sale. *In its entirety.* I would be blessed with the good fortune of writing very large cheques to every member of my executive team as a gesture of appreciation on behalf of the company and Bain. What an experience!

Many of my colleagues at SuperPages Canada decided to make the transition to Yellow Pages Group, and they were rewarded for doing so. I was also asked to stay on, but I made a decision to move a different direction. I was, again, exhausted and I didn't feel that I had the energy to take the company forwards, and watch transformation yet again, less than a year after the initial sale to Bain.

That's when I turned to myself in the mirror and asked, "What's next?" In many ways, this is where the story ends. This is the story of the great transaction that will always be the pinnacle of achievement in my professional career. But it was just the beginning of my awakening, and the start of the rest of my life.

My incredible Bain Capital experience, my journey to Base Camp of Mount Everest with my son, T.J., and all of the ups and downs in my personal and professional life have led me to put together the

Everest Model that you see on the pages of this book: three rules to live by, five principles to be guided by, and six promises to keep.

Boardroom to Base Camp

Life and Leadership Lessons from the Top

EVEREST MODEL

Principle One*: Foundation*

"The loftiest edifices need the deepest foundations."
- George Santayana

The key to my success has been, above all else, belief in myself. This belief is at the very Foundation of every day, every objective, and every journey in life.

When you open your eyes at the beginning of each day, it often takes a moment to be sure of your surroundings (even if you have woken up in the same bed for the last 20 years). Once you have determined where you are, and details of your day's plans start rushing at you from all directions, it's time to think about your Foundation. This is where the start of every journey begins.

Before a developer can start building a skyscraper, he needs to lay a firm Foundation – we need to do the same with our bodies and minds. Instead of "building a tower" from the first moment of your day, checking your emails on your smartphone, eating breakfast and running out the door, see if you can "build a Foundation" first.

Take a look at the Everest Model at the start of this chapter. Start by looking through the outer triangle, made up of the three sides: Yourself, Community and Mission. Remembering these three rules at all times can give you the support that will help you to be successful through the day. By design, "Yourself" is at the base of the triangle, because it represents the Foundation of everything you envision.

1. Say "thank you" because you just opened your eyes, and you have another special day on this Earth. This will help you think of Yourself.

Yourself is the first rule of guidance in day-to-day life. If you haven't grounded yourself and attended to your own needs, you will be in no position to support or contribute effectively to the other components in life. Liken it to strapping your own oxygen mask on before your child's during an emergency in an airplane. There is a good reason that flight attendants tell you to do this! You can't help others unless you take care of yourself first.

I start every day with the word "thanks." Far too often things don't go the way we plan. As I have been writing this book, there was another terrible tragedy on Mount Everest where eight climbers were killed. Life is fragile, and we never know when our last day is going to be. Every day, after we successfully open our eyes, we can start building a strong Foundation by simply saying, "thank you."

2. Remember the Golden Rule. No matter what you do throughout the day, as you

start your journey do unto others as you want done to you. This will remind you of the importance of Community.

When I think of Community, I think of everyone who is important to me at this moment in time. Family, neighbors, friendships and colleagues are all part of that picture. Both you and your community will be stronger by simply remembering and applying the Golden Rule.

I understand this might seem like pretty simple stuff. Most of us had the Golden Rule impressed upon us as we were growing up – I was no different. But later in my life, I realized the great impact of this rule in our lives, and how it truly is the route to all success.

Every group of people on Earth has one way or another of expressing this concept. Here are a few examples. The Golden Thread, as taught in Hinduism, is, "Treat others as you would like to be treated." In Judaism, a similar rule teaches, "What is hurtful to yourself, do not to another." In Taoism, the expression goes, "Hurt not others with that which pains you." Buddhists say, "What you do not desire yourself, do not put before others." Christians repeat, "Do unto others as you would have them do unto you." Muslims say, "Do unto all as you would wish to have done to you." The Golden Rule is simple, and we learn it early in our lives, but it is the most important component of a solid Foundation.

We often think of the Golden Rule as something we do *only* for others. That's not true – we get significant benefits ourselves as well. If you are disciplined enough to apply this rule, you will go through every single day in a much more balanced state. You will enjoy a more solid Foundation as a result, which leads to all future success.

3. The only thing that you have control of is how you react to every situation that comes your way. This will help you to have a Mission.

Our Mission is more than simply our job or career. Your Mission is what you are focused on accomplishing: your goals and objectives, your focused purposes. It is no accident this is the *third* rule. Only *after* you have attended to yourself and your community are you able to successfully move towards the achievement of the Mission.

There may be times that you will be driving along the freeway and someone with road rage will do something crazy. Other times, you will be trekking up a mountain and will see a challenging climb ahead of you. In corporate life, you might be dealing with any number of issues inside your organization, from cash flow to management and employee problems and disputes. The list in corporate life and in life in general is endlessly filled with things that can go wrong.

In any one of these situations, remember that the only thing you are really in control of is how you react. It will make all the difference in the world. I have had the privilege of working with many great leaders who exemplified this trait – always being in control of how they react. It is absolutely crystal clear to me that being around competent individuals who stay in control will avoid the pitfalls of success: fear, threats, and embarrassment.

If you apply the three simple Rules of Yourself, Community, and Mission to each day of your personal and business life, you will find balance and strength. With a great deal of hard work, that will lead you to the top. More importantly, it will lead you to whatever or wherever *your* top is.

These three simple reminders at the start of every day, and these three rules of discipline can provide a strong Foundation beneath you. However, beware of pouring the concrete of your Foundation properly! Just as pouring concrete appears simple at first, if you haven't mixed it properly and poured when the conditions are right, you run the risk of problems later in the project, or during the next steps of the Everest Model. Take the time to be disciplined in pouring the right Foundation before you move on.

At the beginning of our preparation for Mount Everest Base Camp, T.J. and I also had to build a Foundation. We had to ground ourselves in the belief that we could accomplish this, and we had to commit ourselves to the task ahead. We weren't going to be climbing to the summit of Everest, but we still were taking a very long journey to just under 19,000 feet where Base Camp is located.

We thought about ourselves first. Were we in good enough shape? How did we feel about the trip? What did we need to do to get ready?

Then T.J. and I thought about Community. From the beginning, community meant the two of us, but it also meant our family surrounding us, and our friends supporting us. Once the trip began, it also meant our fellow trekkers.

Lastly, we thought about our Mission – once we had a handle on ourselves, and felt surrounded by Community, we were able to start our Mission.

Barbra, being the thrifty and careful spender she always has been, decided to book our flight from Calgary through Frankfurt, into Delhi, and on to Kathmandu. As a travel tip for any Canadians reading this, traveling east towards Kathmandu is probably not the most advisable way to go. However, there was clearly an opportunity for savings by traveling in that direction, and I guess that was a key ingredient to Barb's Foundation. It was an incredibly lengthy flight, but our adventure had just begun.

T.J. and I were very committed to our journey. However, when you have Commitment, one of the three key ingredients to a solid Foundation, it doesn't mean that you have all the answers. When T.J. and I were about to leave Canada, we were confident that we had done all we could with respect to the research, and we were committed to the objective as the journey began. But we can never have all the answers, and, clearly, as I jumped on the plane, I had thoughts and questions in my mind.

If you avoid Commitment because you fear you don't have all the answers, beware! You might actually find yourself in a frozen state of fear (one of the pitfalls of success).

We soon arrived in Kathmandu, an incredible and unique place. We were in wonder at the city's strange beauty – yet within this beauty there was so much poverty. I thought perhaps it was only to my North American eyes, but the city seemed to be in chaos, with people racing all over the place. It was as if we were in a movie: motorcycles, cars, pedestrians, and tables set up, selling everything imaginable, from raw fish to chicken in the heat of the day. I started to question my reality. *What is this place? What are we doing here?*

As we spoke about our observations, a new local friend explained what we were seeing. He told us that chaos was understandable, given the fact that the royal family that used to govern Nepal had been assassinated less than ten years prior. Since then, they had been trying to form a democratic government with the participation of 28 major political parties. That was unimaginable to even comprehend: 28 different parties trying to agree on a direction. I had previously thought the Canadian political system was strained with its four major parties – certainly not, compared with this.

As we sat there in this strange place, I thought to myself, *How do you fix something like this?* Our friend seemed to read my mind, and he looked at me straight in the eyes and said, "The world cannot have what you have." This was such a stark contrast to what the Boston businessman had said to me at the 2005 celebration: "It's never enough."

Thinking about my own journey up the corporate ladder, and all of the corporate grooming that clearly would contradict a statement that suggested mediocrity was acceptable, I said to our Nepalese friend, "I believe that if you have ambition and dreams, you can go after anything you want in life. It just takes goals and a plan."

He replied very simply, "No, the world cannot provide for what you in North America have."

It took me a little while to realize it, but he was right. There are not enough resources to give to everyone in the world what we on the North American continent have. All it takes is simple math. Add up the sum of natural resources North Americans consume, and divide that by the small fraction of the world's population North Americans comprise. It is clear that the planet does not have enough resources to provide North American consumption levels to everyone across the world.

I understood our friend's message, and it hit me hard. He repeated, "If you think that there's enough abundance in the world to give everyone what you have, you are wrong."

We had scarcely begun our adventure, and I had already learned my first great lesson. We so often take for granted our political and social structures here in North America. We have an incredible Foundation, and need to be thankful for the support it gives us in our personal and business lives.

I learned a significant lesson that day as a result of this honest man's brief introduction to Nepal. When I finally listened and allowed myself to open up to his wisdom, I understood.

Whether you are starting out in business and challenging yourself to accomplish grandiose tasks, or starting on your journey up to Base Camp Mount Everest, you better make sure that you have a strong Foundation. As chaotic as Kathmandu is, that city is the beginning point of every Everest journey. Out of the chaos of that city, we met our guide, gathered our supplies, and were able to start on our journey. You can do the same with your life and your business.

Despite what might often seem like the chaos of Kathmandu around you, this is the Foundation of everything to come. If you start with a belief in yourself, a commitment to the journey and the integrity to get things done, you will be able to accomplish your mission with your community around you, despite the chaos.

In your mind, picture the Foundation of a skyscraper and then Mount Everest. What is the difference between them? Which would you rather be?

A mountain has a solid, strong, wide base – enabling it to reach thousands of meters into the sky. A tower, on the other hand, is very narrow, and might have a strong foundation, but cannot possibly compete with a mountain's strength.

Once you look at each day through the solid, foundational, mountain-like triangle of Yourself, Community and Mission, your journey towards the top begins with the first principle, Foundation. The three ingredients of Foundation are: Commitment, Integrity and Belief.

1. Be committed to believing in yourself, through thick and thin. This isn't always easy – and we can often be our own worst enemies. Think about your ultimate goals, and develop a positive attitude towards achieving your mission. Find the value in everything and every relationship, and reaffirm your commitments to each. Most importantly, try thinking about commitment like the following equation.

Commitment = Desire + Plan + Persistence + Belief + Attitude

2. Second, your word is everything. Do everything you can to speak with clarity

and precision, and to stick to exactly what you say. No one is perfect, but you can build incredible relationships if you simply stand by your word. Also, never make assumptions about people or situations. You will be wrong! And work hard each day to be the best at whatever you do.

3. Third, be able to state your deepest beliefs for people. What principles and values do you live by? Remember to believe in yourself – that is the key to achieving your mission. Finally, remember that those who think they can, do.

Our ability to deliver on any objective in front of us starts with our belief that *we can do it*. People throughout recent history have referred to this concept in many ways. Charles Swindoll spoke and wrote about "attitude", Napoleon Hill wrote about "the law of attraction", and the recent movie and book "The Secret" refers to this same concept. The way I like to think about this is that you will *get back* what you *put out*.

Think about the key ingredient to *putting out* the right stuff. If you start from a position of unbelief, or with a poor attitude, or with a *can't*-mindset, guess where you will end up? Probably with another missed objective and plenty of disappointment.

This is simple, but hard at the same time. I have had many misses in my life, and have not achieved every target. One thing that I can say with certainty is that I have never *achieved* something or *hit* my target without first *believing* that I would be able to accomplish my objective.

Write the following phrase on your mirror, refrigerator, wall, or anywhere you will see it regularly:

"The key to my success is belief in myself."

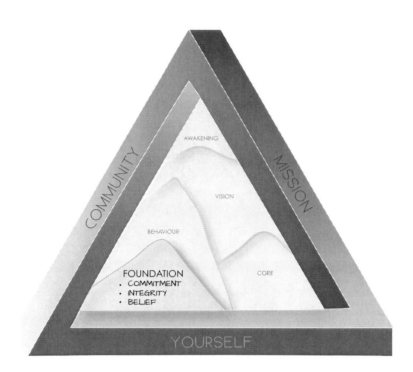

FOUNDATION
Ingredient #1: Commitment

- The key to success is belief in yourself, and commitment to that belief.
- Approach all of your goals with a positive, yet realistic, attitude.
- Reaffirm your commitments.
- Are you using the commitment formula?

Commitment = Desire + Plan + Persistence + Belief + Attitude

APPLICATIONS – *COMMITMENT*

1. List a few of your deepest beliefs here:

Professional Beliefs	*Personal Beliefs*
_____	_____
_____	_____
_____	_____

2. In what ways are you committed to those beliefs?

_____

_____

3. What are some of your goals & what is your mission?

Short-Term Goals	*Overall Mission*
_____	_____
_____	_____
_____	_____

4. What are some of your commitments and how can you reaffirm them?

_____

_____

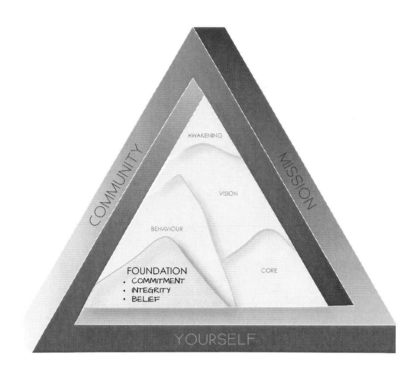

FOUNDATION
Ingredient #2: Integrity

- Your word is everything. Speak with clarity and precision, and stick to what you say.
- Never make assumptions. You will be wrong!
- Be the best at whatever you do.
- Let go of your ego – it is never personal.

APPLICATIONS – *INTEGRITY*

1. List some examples of how your *word* is important:

  Personal Life   *Professional Life*

  _____   _____

  _____   _____

  _____   _____

2. How can you speak with more clarity and precision?

_____

_____

3. List some assumptions you have made in the past.

  Personal Life   *Professional Life*

  _____   _____

  _____   _____

  _____   _____

4. Are there ways you can be better at what you do?

_____

_____

_____

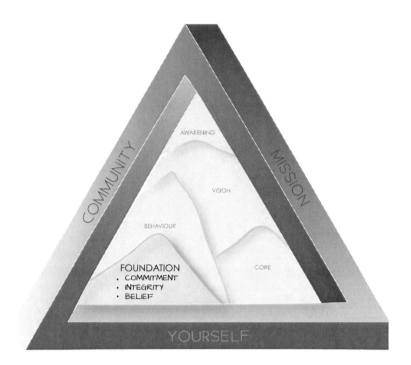

FOUNDATION
Ingredient #3: Belief

- Be able to state the most important beliefs, principles and values that you live by.
- Those who think they can, do.
- Believe in yourself – that is the key to your goals.

"Believe in yourself and the world will believe in you."

– Jim Oleson

APPLICATIONS – *BELIEF*

1. What are some of your key principles or values?

       Personal Life   *Professional Life*

       _____   _____

       _____   _____

       _____   _____

2. How can you better express those principles to others?

_____

_____

3. How can you have a stronger belief in yourself?

       Personal Life   *Professional Life*

       _____   _____

       _____   _____

       _____   _____

4. How will believing more in yourself change things?

_____

_____

When I started climbing up the corporate ladder, I was at the very bottom. That's the way it usually is. The first boardroom I ever entered was at Canadian Tire Petroleum.

I was the youngest of twelve District Managers in the Division. In fact, most of them were at least a decade older than I was. It was an intimating environment, to say the least, but I was youthful, inquisitive and full of drive to succeed. That was my Foundation.

When you start climbing Mount Everest, you have to start in Kathmandu, a city that is the starting point (and Foundation) of every climb to Mount Everest Base Camp (or beyond). Despite the "cracks" in the "Foundation" of Kathmandu, your journey must start here.

From this position, we need to strengthen our Foundation. Let's think about a house. If you have a strong Foundation, just about anything else can be fixed. Mistakes and deficiencies you discover in other parts of the building can be repaired, but the foundation must remain strong and intact.

If you discover that you have cracks in your Foundation, don't despair. With plenty of hard work, persistence, and by using the three Ingredients of the first Principle (Commitment, Integrity, and Belief), you can repair the Foundation. But if you are just building the Foundation, take care to do it the right way the first time around!

Start slow, with simple steps, and you can pick up speed later on. Each morning, remember to start with *Yourself* before you move on to other things. Don't keep your smartphone near your bedside – why does it have to be the first thing you look at in the morning? Instead, look over at your spouse, scratch your dog's chin, or step outside for a look at the sunrise. Take a few moments to build your Foundation for the day.

The same thing applies to work. When you step through the door of your office, don't immediately dive into your pile of emails. Start with *Yourself*, thinking about your workspace, your mood and your day's schedule. Then think about your *Community*, and enjoy a positive morning meeting with your team. At that meeting, think about your *Mission*, and your goals for the day, the week, and the quarter.

Make healthy choices, get plenty of rest, and surround yourself with the right people. You are a product of your environment, and if they are healthy, you will also be healthy. Also, don't underestimate the value of your physical well-being. If you are not looking after yourself with physical activity, the right amount of rest and everything in moderation, you are not setting yourself up to have a strong Foundation. And lace up your hiking boots, because you're headed up Everest.

APPLICATIONS – *FOUNDATION*

1. What is the first thing you usually do when you get out of bed in the morning?

_____

_____

2. What do you do when you arrive at your office?

_____

_____

3. What actions could help you build your *Foundation?*

Personal Life	*Professional Life*
_____	_____
_____	_____
_____	_____

4. What will you try to do/say from now on when you get out of bed in the morning and when you arrive at the office?

_____

_____

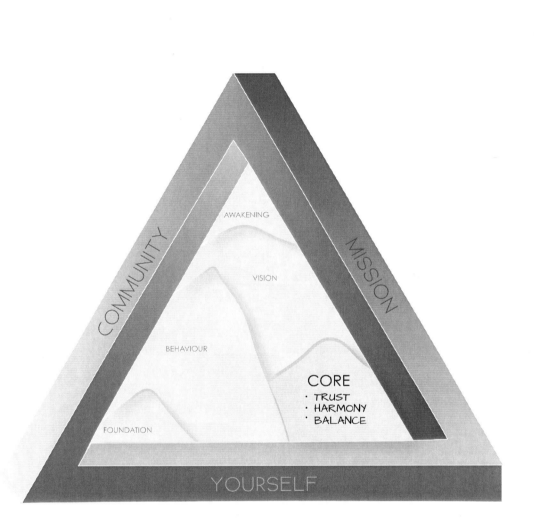

EVEREST MODEL
Principle Two: Core

"At the core of life is a hard purposefulness,
a determination to live."
- Howard Thurman

It became apparent to me very early in my life that I needed to have a strong Core. This isn't too far away from the concept of Core that professional athletes and trainers talk about; a solid Core in your body helps you to be stable in every aspect of your life.

Picture in your mind an extremely fit individual you might see on an exercise program – you know what I mean, that individual with six-pack abs of steel. Focus solely on their Core – don't look at their arms or their legs – just their Core. It's incredibly strong. I liken that strength to the requirement of strength required in the Everest model in the second Principle: Core. What are workout requirements or exercises you need to participate in to achieve the strength of this Core? There are three Ingredients: Trust, Harmony, and Balance.

This is how I want you to see the Core of Yourself, your Community and your Mission. Don't worry about the appendages for now. You have a strong Foundation, and now you are focusing on the Core.

This Core is made up of the ultimate ingredients of strength: trust, harmony and balance.

1. Trust is an ingredient that is vitally important to every team – think of a trust fall: if one person neglects to catch the falling person, the whole team fails. And if the falling person doesn't trust that his coworkers will catch him, they won't succeed in their task.

When I was with my son, T.J., in the Himalayan mountains, we had to trust each other fully. It's the same way in the boardroom – my executive team at SuperPages Canada had to trust me as their leader, and I had to trust them. We were a new team. We had new direction and to a certain degree new energy. All the things we had discussed we would do if only we could were suddenly available to us. Trust was extremely important in determining our direction and solidifying our ideas: trust between my team and me, and between Bain and us. It was incredibly important to our survival and our success.

Trust is also incredibly critical in our families and in our workplaces. Without trust you have very little chance of success, either personally or professionally. We are all human and from time to time we may jeopardize trust, but it is important to remember that if trust is ever broken, it can be repaired. In other words, if we can avoid putting ourselves in situations where trust *has* to be repaired, we will be far better off.

2. Harmony is what every team needs to work together. Think of a symphony, and how all of the instruments work together to make a complex piece of music sound like it comes from one unified voice.

To play on this comparison of the symphony, think of the conductor (the leader), the choir (all of the employees), the lead vocalist (the management) and the various musicians (critical departments). If they are not in harmony, you have a real problem. There is nothing worse than the musicians and the vocalist not being in sync with one another.

We could also look to team sports to see harmony at its best. Since I have refereed thousands of youth hockey games, I'll use a hockey analogy. Look at the Los Angeles Kings, the hockey team that was an underdog in the National Hockey League until it won the Stanley Cup Championship in 2012 for the first time in its history. The team was made up of several good players but very few superstars. However, they synchronized with one another in all aspects of the game. That is harmony – working incredibly well together in a team environment toward a common goal. Each of them knew what their role was, and how and when they had to do things.

3. Balance is something we see mountain climbers and gymnasts use to great advantage. All of our lives are like that – we are balancing on top of a cornice, between family and work.

Balance in life and in work is unbelievably critical. I have coached many CEOs, business leaders and individuals, and they all tell me the importance of balance in life. Yet very few of them can demonstrate success in this area. Nearly without fail, the words I hear are, "I have no time for myself after work and family."

Follow the Everest Model and you will realize the following: first, they have it backward (Yourself, then Community and then Mission is the optimal order for Balance), and second, there is a way to accomplish Balance and build on a solid Core if you are disciplined with your time. Later I will have you complete an exercise to get you started.

When we focus on the Core of our team at work, we don't often think of our own needs. We are no longer talking about what you do when you wake up in the morning. We are talking about when you go home at night, whether you go to your kids' hockey games or activities. Do you spend quality time with your family? Do you spend time with yourself? Is there any spiritual time?

Why do we often simply *talk* about Balance, but we don't create an environment that helps us to be successful in this area? You need to *actively* make Balance a priority in your personal and professional life, and encourage everyone around you to make it a priority as well. Balance is a vital ingredient of a solid Core.

If every member of your team is internally balanced, your community team dynamic will be well balanced as well, and you will have more success than you could have ever imagined.

When I was a child, my parents might not have used the words Balance and Harmony, but they certainly used the word *Trust*. In fact, trust was the absolute common thread in our home. It was instinctive in the environment we grew up in. You would trust that others would honor the Golden Rule if you did. They would treat you as they wanted to be treated. You trusted that you would respect one another.

I think it's fairly logical to assume that successful families have Trust: they have Trust among themselves and they are honest with one another. If Trust isn't absolutely second nature within the home, you're going to have an awful lot of misunderstandings and possibly even animosity.

Again, Trust is built by what you *do*, not simply what you say. When you are working in an organization (whether a large or small company), the group you work with becomes a "family," and the harmony among the members of that group is critical to their ultimate success.

Our families go through tough times and challenges just as our teams at work do. Think about it – you are living together for an extended period of time. Can you imagine doing that with colleagues? This is not an easy thing to do!

It takes real work for husbands and wives to live together in Harmony. They often have conflicting issues – coming home from the work environment and approaching one another with the challenges of the day. How do you disconnect from that and re-engage inside the family environment? Again you have to try to do that in a harmonious fashion.

I see there as being two harmonic rules to having a successful and happy family life, and you can apply the same questions to the successful start of a new career. These are basically two Harmony questions that you need to ask yourself.

1. Where do you want to go on the journey of life?

2. With whom do you want to travel on that journey?

You cannot reverse the two questions. They have to be answered in this order. If you reverse them, you are going to get yourself in a heck of a lot of trouble, and you may not find yourself in a harmonious state. This is the same in business, on Everest, and everywhere else.

Think hard for a moment about the first question above. Where do you plan on going with your life? If your desire is to end up retired in a cottage on a lake, and your spouse's plan is to end up someday in a condo in a major urban center, you are in trouble. This is why you have to answer this question first. If you have a different destination than your partners, either at home or at work, you are going to have trouble. That is the essence of Harmony in the Everest Model.

Let's apply this to career changes instead of relationships. When you are thinking about a change of employment or career, first ask yourself the two Harmony questions. Next, review what I call the *Six Primary Satisfiers of Work.*

1. Does the work fit my competency?
2. Does the compensation meet my expectations?
3. Is there growth here?
4. Will I fit in and be accepted?
5. Do I have common values and principles?
6. Will I have good work/home Balance?

Although people of my parents' generation didn't use the word Balance very often, they practiced it in many ways – and it deeply involved Harmony and Trust. People would work from nine to five with a clear Mission – to work hard until closing time, and then come home to a Harmonious life. Too often, in our workplace and at home, we don't feel that same Balance. As a result, our Core is weak.

As simplistic as this may sound, taking these three ingredients of Core into the business arena, whether you are a leader or a team member, and applying them in every one of your discussions, your communication style, and your actions, will ultimately create a more successful venture and adventure for everyone.

This was uncharted territory for T.J. and me. We didn't know what the next day was going to bring. We had no idea. We had a rough idea in terms of the map that we were traveling on so we had a little bit of a plan, but neither T.J. nor I had ever traveled these steps before. We had an incredible guide for our entire journey on the mountain, but we still had to take those steps ourselves. Sir Edmund Hillary was the same way when he climbed Everest the first time in 1953 – he had the help of guide Tenzing Norgay, but he had to take each step and breathe each breath himself in order to make it to the top of the world successfully.

The same way that Norgay and Hillary had to trust one another, T.J. and I had to trust each other. We weren't risking our lives to the same degree as the two Everest pioneers had done, but we certainly put ourselves at risk several times during the journey. And we couldn't have made it if we hadn't trusted one another, worked in harmony together, and focused on our physical and mental balance.

We had to trust one another and be honest when we were experiencing symptoms of altitude sickness. We had to be honest with each other as we thought about fatigue. We had to believe in one another – the ultimate belief that only comes as a result of trust.

T.J, and I would be flying aboard a DeHavilland Canada Twin Otter to Lukla. I was happy to hear and see that the airplane was neither rickety nor old, and, hey, it was Canadian, *eh?* So I didn't have any fears until I did a search of online videos, and discovered that Lukla, a city in northeastern Nepal, had one of the most dangerous landing strips in the world. You can likewise search online and check it out – I recommend it. The planes land on a runway uphill, and at the end is a mountain wall.

Despite my anxiety, we landed successfully, and that's where our journey to Mount Everest Base Camp began in earnest.

The first day, a five-hour hike didn't get us much further towards our goal of just under 19,000 feet – Mount Everest Base Camp. Nonetheless, our journey over what would be the next 18 days, with approximately 28 hours of trekking and ascents and descents had begun. What a thrill it was, as we started our Day One journey towards the village of Phakding.

Much to my surprise, we started our first day at 9,000 feet and ended the day at 8,000 feet. I am no mathematician, but I know this wasn't good progress! The realization of trekking in the Himalayan Mountains was setting in – sometimes you have to go down in order to go up towards your goal.

Over the next three days, we worked hard to start climbing a few feet in altitude, and we eventually hit the Namche Grunt. Our guides and others told us that the Namche Grunt would probably be the toughest day we would experience. I would later realize there were many more *grunts* to follow. We climbed 2,000 feet on a nearly-60-degree slope. It was a painstaking grind: anything steeper would have required ropes.

As challenging as the Namche Grunt was, it clearly put many things into perspective with regards to the importance of a strong Core. We had to leave our ego off the mountain, and Trust in the journey, Trust our guides and Trust our fellow trekkers. This wasn't a time to overreact. We needed to stay in Harmony with our surroundings and make sure we had the right balance both physically and mentally.

When we got to the top of Namache Bazar, we were at 11,000 feet – already the highest altitude I had ever physically travelled to in my life. The plan was to stay for a couple of days, primarily to acclimate to the altitude; it was vitally important that we be aware of the effects high altitude could have on us. Our great fear was altitude sickness, which was very common, and if you weren't careful, could be life-threatening. Symptoms would include things like vomiting, loss of appetite, headaches, major headaches and something called "chain stoking," which basically means that you feel like you're suffocating while lying in a resting position. We had read a good amount about altitude sickness in preparing for our journey, and were prepared in some ways. But it was daunting to be resting at 11,000 feet,

thinking about the fact that we had to become ac-
climated before climbing any higher.

Later on in our journey, when, at a much higher
altitude in Lobuche, I thought I was going to die
because of chain stoking, I wrote a journal entry to
Barbra, just in case. I was lying one night next to T.J.
on a simple piece of plywood, and I couldn't breathe.
I didn't want to wake him, so I wrote. But having
him there made a huge difference in my recovery
over the next few days.

T.J. and I had to be harmonious. We were working
with (formerly) complete strangers, trekking up the
side of the tallest mountain in the world. We had to
work together, or we could find ourselves in terrible
trouble.

What do I mean by harmonious? I see harmony taking shape on any team through three keys, stem-
ming from the Golden Rule. These keys worked on
the mountain, and they worked in the boardroom.

1. Treat others as *you* would like to be treated.

2. Be *nice* to people.

3. Work *with* people towards solutions.

I know – these three keys seem ridiculously simple.
But we often forget some of the simplest things
when we are in community with other people, espe-

cially when we are challenged, or, on Everest, when the oxygen is low.

Having the incredible opportunity to spend time in the Himalayan Mountains also taught me about the importance of simplicity in this way: the villages of the Sherpa people are very simple, but they are immensely harmonious. This Harmony hit me straight in the forehead – I will never forget it.

One day as we were trekking towards Dingboche, we stopped in a very small village for a rest and some Sherpa Tea. This special tea – a concoction made from tea, milk and sugar, had become something we looked forward to everywhere we stopped. I seemed to recall my mother making a variation of this same drink when I was young, although she called it "Angel Tea." Anyway, as we sat drinking our tea, we watched a young mother wash some clothing on a rock in a nearby stream of water. Immediately behind her, older kids were playing a game. Everyone seemed completely relaxed and very happy, all of them going about their daily activities in absolute Harmony with everything. It was one of those moments where we realized how few material things people truly needed to be content.

As we left that village and its extremely peaceful surroundings, I realized the entire journey so far had the same ingredients as what I just witnessed. As we trekked we were able to balance on the edge of crevasses and on the side of steep cliffs because we worked together with our guides in harmony, and we trusted them completely. This was the Core of our experience together as we journeyed through the

Himalayan Mountains and ventured up to Base Camp at just under 19,000 feet.

There is absolutely no question that the success I enjoyed inside of various boardrooms had the ingredients of Trust, Harmony and Balance. On top of the strong Foundation my executive teams and I built, we worked hard to bake the three ingredients of Core into every interaction.

I have often been asked about my own contribution to the success of Bain's largest private equity transaction within a seven-month period. My simple answer is that we assembled the right team. When I think back on my team's hugely successful effort at Bain Capital, I am extremely proud. So, how did we build a fantastic team? It all comes back to a strong Core.

We assembled a team within the framework of Bain Capital that had the ingredient of Trust. We had absolute Trust in every person involved. It was not easy to build or maintain that Trust, but it was incredibly important to the Core of our Community and our Mission.

There was a clear consensus in the boardroom during that venture. We all knew that we were going to be tackling challenging issues and sensitive topics in our work together. We went through exercises to make sure that we established Trust with one another in order to work on those issues and topics.

While working to foster Trust between our team members, we were also promoting Harmony. We created a workplace where everyone involved had a desire to work with one another. Sure, there were plenty of awkward moments where various team members would challenge one another, but at the end of the day, they understood what each one of their roles were, and how they were going to work together. They knew that we were all going to strive towards the success of rebuilding SuperPages Canada into an incredibly successful privately held company. That was our challenge, since the company came from a very traditional corporate public environment – and we faced it head on, with determination.

Let's go back to the athletic analogy now – talking about the Core of your body. It's great to have strong legs, but every single exercise you do in life, whether it be leg exercises, working your biceps or doing pushups, ultimately you will need a strong Core: both externally and internally. So, how do you build that strength?

When you work with your team (or your family) through the ingredients of Trust, Harmony and Balance, you also need to be well aligned from a values perspective. This leads us back to the three sides of the Everest triangle: Yourself, Community and Mission.

First, in order to strengthen your Core, you have to believe in Yourself. Think of this as something like "sit-ups for your soul." You don't need a six-pack to have strong abs. You just need to do those sit-ups every day. You need to take care of yourself and your own needs first.

Next, approach everything you do in your Community with a giving attitude. Understand that it truly is better to give than receive. Avoid participating in what I call "a disposable society."

We live in a world where everything just seems to be disposable these days. When my parents were growing up, if the toaster broke, they would have to fix it. In our world today, we throw the toaster out without even considering repair.

Using that same example of the broken toaster, let's make it our renewed Mission to never give up. Why throw the toaster out when you can fix it? When things go wrong with our relationships and our teams, we should work to fix them, and not just throw them away and move on.

Think about your Mission as you move forwards, and don't subscribe to the disposable society. Look at ways that you can participate in your Community with the strong attribute of giving – you will see a world of difference.

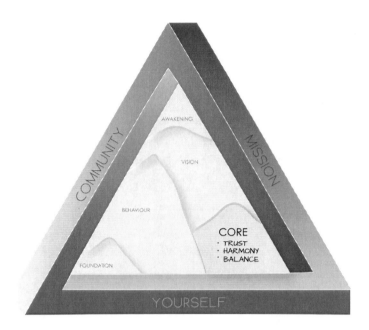

CORE
Ingredient #1: Trust

- Everyone starts at neutral. Only when you start talking will you go up or down from there.
- Trust is everything!
- Be honest. Always.
- If you cannot be honest, shut up!
- You can repair trust, but for every step backwards, you will need to move two forwards.

APPLICATIONS – *TRUST*

1. List a few people/companies you trust:

Companies you trust   *People you trust*

_____   _____

_____   _____

_____   _____

2. What are some reasons you trust those people/companies?

_____

_____

3. When have you broken someone else's trust?

At Home   *At Work*

_____   _____

_____   _____

_____   _____

4. What steps can you take to repair trust when it has been broken? How could you have kept trust intact?

_____

_____

CORE
Ingredient #2: Harmony

- Teamwork begins with the right surroundings. Make sure that you build the right environment.
- Look around the room. Are your values aligned with the people around you?
- If you don't think you fit in, you usually don't.
- Look around the room again. If you can learn something, stay!

APPLICATIONS – *HARMONY*

1. What does the right environment look like for you?

At home   *At work*

_____   _____

_____   _____

_____   _____

2. What are a few situations where you don't fit in?

_____

_____

3. With whom do your values align best?

At Home   *At Work*

_____   _____

_____   _____

_____   _____

4. How can you spend more time with those who align with your values, both personally and at work?

_____

_____

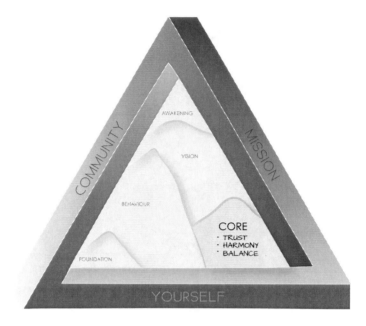

CORE
Ingredient #3: Balance

- 50/50 doesn't exist. Sometimes you will give 60%, and sometimes 40%. Balance means that half the time you will be at 40% and the other half of the time at 60%!
- Try to always make decisions with the following three things in mind (in this order):
    1. Yourself
    2. Community
    3. Mission

Self + Community + Mission + Social + Spiritual = 168 hours

APPLICATIONS – *BALANCE*

1. Take the 168 hours in a week, and break them down into the following five categories (see the equation on the previous page). When you are calculating the number of total hours in your week, remember to first calculate your sleep time by removing the hours you *must* sleep per week. (Many studies suggest that adults require 7.5-9 hours per night).

SELF _____ hours

COMMUNITY _____ hours

MISSION _____ hours

SOCIAL _____ hours

SPIRITUAL _____ hours

_____

HOURS IN YOUR WEEK   168 - ___ = ___ hours

2. Now take the same 168 hours in each week, and think about your "ideal" week. This is the way you want your life balance to work. Break your time down into the following five categories. *(Always allocate hours in this order!)*

SELF _____ hours

COMMUNITY _____ hours

MISSION _____ hours

SOCIAL _____ hours

SPIRITUAL _____ hours

_____

HOURS IN YOUR WEEK   168 - ___ = ___ hours

The process of strengthening our Core requires an incredibly focused effort, but it is ultimately worthwhile. Take my word for it! I saw a strong Core paying off both in the boardroom and on my journey to Base Camp. Here are a few reminders of how to build your Core:

- Work hard to align your values with your everyday activities and actions.

- Believe in Yourself – this will greatly strengthen your Core beliefs and values.

- Have a spirit of giving. This is one of the surest signs of a strong and stable Core.

- Avoid participating in the "disposable" aspects of society, instead focusing on things that matter to your Community and Mission.

After having built a supportive Foundation and a strong Core, the next step will be to look at Behaviour, through the ingredients of Resolve, Virtue and Focus.

APPLICATIONS – *CORE*

1. What kind of Core exercises have you used at the gym? How could those same principles apply to your work?

_____

_____

2. Can you think of ways to strengthen the Core of your corporate team and your family life?

_____

_____

3. What actions could help you build your *Core?*

      Personal Life   *Professional Life*

      _____   _____

      _____   _____

      _____   _____

4. How will you look towards the future with a focus on the things that matter most to you?

_____

_____

EVEREST MODEL

Principle Three: *Behaviour*

"Behaviour is the mirror in which everyone shows their image."
- Johann Wolfgang von Goethe

Your actions speak louder than words – these were words I was groomed with as I grew up. These same words followed me in and out of boardrooms throughout my career.

Was I the model kid? Well, not really – who is? But whether I displayed good behaviour or bad behaviour, the most important thing was what I *learned* from those Behaviours. We have to learn from the actions we take in our lives, and then make change happen where it is needed.

In other words, whether you're leading a company or participating in a family, and there's suddenly some kind of "bad" Behaviour, the most important thing is what you do *afterwards*. It doesn't ultimately matter whether what you did was right or wrong. It matters what you did after the fact. Think back on your life, and you will see that is the case nearly all of the time.

The worst way to try to have "good" Behaviour is to think that we will never make mistakes. That just won't happen. We are flawed as humans, and we can't ever change that. But we *will* be judged on how we change after we make those mistakes, or display bad Behaviour.

Behaviour is certainly not as concrete as the two other principles, Foundation and Core, but it's the principle that probably makes the most impact on how you will be judged by others.

What kind of attitude do you exude? What's the image that you're portraying? What's the air about you? Behaviour is somewhat intangible in this way – very hard to *measure* – but very easy to *see*.

When you think about leadership, whether you might be leading a company, managing a group of individuals in a company, being an individual that is walking up to Base Camp, or a family member – what are the qualities that you think a leader should demonstrate and exude?

I see it this way. When you see someone who is a model leader with excellent behaviour, you will feel something. You will say to yourself, "I'd like to be more like that."

Beyond that characterization, I see model leaders behaving in a way that doesn't have a lot of ego. They might be someone who has a positive attitude, or a high tolerance level for critical feedback. Their qualities are apparent and not hidden. There is transparency in everything they do. They are open in everything they do, and display the most important ingredients of Behaviour: Resolve, Virtue and Focus.

What does "good" Behaviour look like? We know how schoolchildren are supposed to act. But what about Behaviour in the workplace and at home? Here are two ways to see what your ROI (return on investment) from exemplary Behaviour might look like.

1. If you are "doing unto others", as the Golden Rule suggests, then your Behaviour will be well-rewarded in terms of your interaction with the Community, and your eventual impact on the Mission.

2. If you are treating people with respect, whether you are leading a company towards its Mission or interacting within your Community, guess what will come right back at you? Exactly what you put in – people who treat you with respect.

If you have the right Behaviours just as my team did inside the Bain Capital boardroom, and just as T.J. and I did as we climbed up Everest, good things will come back to you. And, yes, it is that simple.

What I am telling you, and the common theme we will always come back to throughout this book, is that *simplicity* is vitally important. Each principle in the Everest Model reinforces this. The principles are simple, yet they take great discipline to accomplish.

T.J. and I were used to being around tall mountains. In western Canada, the Rocky Mountains stretch out almost to our back door. However, these mountains are in the range of 10,000-16,000 feet tall. Now, T.J. and I were standing at 16,000 feet, and we were staring up at mountains that were another 12,000-13,000 feet higher. It was an incredibly humbling experience.

Tall peaks were far from the only humbling part of our journey. After working for Bain Capital, I was used to staying at five-star hotels, but "roughing it" was still in my vocabulary. However, the conditions T.J. and I had on Everest were in a different category altogether – they forever redefined "roughing it" for both of us. Suffice to say, our beds didn't have feather pillows with mints on top.

We were blessed to stay in shelters – that's the incredible thing of trekking where so many trekkers have gone before. But those shelters were quite primitive. Each night we would stay in a little lodge. Sometimes the situation could be romantic, like in a Disney film about a trek – where a group of trekkers would huddle together around a stove in the evening and play cards. However, unlike in a film, we had the benefit of a sense of smell, and the yak patties we were burning didn't smell too pleasant.

Every day, we would eat anything that we could boil or fry, so that we wouldn't possibly contract any sickness from what we were eating. That could be disastrous. Luckily, we never experienced something like that.

T.J. and I were part of an adventure together, but it certainly was no vacation. A few trekkers who started the journey with us quit after the first few days, because the conditions were simply too uncomfortable. You can have Virtue, but if you do not have the Focus or the Resolve to get to Base Camp, you will not accomplish the objective. That is also true with all plans and objectives in life. If we don't have the Focus and Resolve, we simply won't get things accomplished.

We worked together with great Focus. We were vigilant in all aspects of our journey, being conscious of what we ate, getting rest, and watching out for one another.

T.J. and I had the Resolve to continue putting one foot after another, all the way up the mountain to Base Camp – higher than either of us had ever been before. Even when we didn't feel comfortable, we continued on with our Focus. I was singularly amazed by my son's Virtue on our journey – and his Resolve and Focus to continue on despite what happened at Lobuche, around 16,000 feet.

Lobuche was where I had experienced chain stoking. I couldn't sleep. I had the terrible feeling of inability to breathe while I was in a resting position. T.J. woke that morning with a headache.

That morning was to be our final push to Base Camp, and then back down to Lobuche. It would be a long, grueling day as we finally met our goal and started our journey home.

Our day began like the rest, other than the lack of sleep for me, and T.J.'s still-mild headache. In hindsight we should have waited another day before the final push. But we were very close to Base Camp, and eager to achieve our objective. We were, in fact, only a mile away, when T.J. started to feel the dramatic effects of altitude sickness.

We were walking on a narrow path up the mountain, and we could see ice fields stretching off into the horizon. Far in the distance, we began to see small little specks – yellow and orange and green tents, all scattered around Mount Everest Base Camp.

As we got closer and closer, T.J. was in a lot of pain, and I grew very concerned about my son's wellbeing.

I turned to T.J., and I said, "I think we should just call it quits and turn around." I tried to say this to him in a way that didn't make him feel like we were admitting defeat. But it seemed to come across to him that way.

T.J. looked at me and pulled a distinct brightness into his eyes. He said, with all of the conviction he could muster, "No, Dad. We have to carry on. We have to push forward."

I will never forget this moment in my life. I knew there was no arguing with T.J. He was going to give this last mile every ounce of his strength. I agreed, and told him that I would be there to support him with each step.

T.J. and I both knew that if we quit or turned around that I would never see Base Camp, and he might not either. So we forged ahead. We arrived at Base Camp and we smiled as a fellow trekker took our photograph. Father and son reached incredible heights that day. But our day wasn't over yet.

T.J. was not in a good place. I have since talked with several friends in the medical profession, and they have explained to me how serious his condition was. I am just happy and grateful to this day that we were able to get T.J. off the mountain.

T.J.'s condition began to worsen as we headed back towards Lobuche. At 17,000 feet, we needed to explore all of our options. I will admit that I was scared. T.J. was weak – he had a pounding headache and was vomiting.

We finally arrived in Gorak Shep, a little village halfway down to Lobuche from Base Camp. At that point, T.J. was getting worse quickly. Although we were starting to descend, we hadn't descended enough for the effects of the altitude to lessen very much. Fatigue was overtaking his body.

I knew I had to do something, and, with the help of our guide, we negotiated a deal with a local, and I acquired a horse (for about $150 U.S. dollars) that T.J. would be able to ride as one of our Sherpa guides led him down the mountain to Lobuche. I knew nightfall was coming, and there was no other way to get him to lower altitude and begin his recovery from altitude sickness.

The next day, because of the lower elevation of Lobuche, and a good night's rest, T.J. was able to trek down the mountain by my side. The effects of his sickness were lessening, but not totally gone. As we continued down the mountain, T.J. was finally able to get back to his "normal" self.

T.J. had shown incredible strength and Behaviour. I was a proud father that day. He and I had gone together to one of the highest points in the world, and now we were headed triumphantly home.

We trek up "mountains" each day in our home and business lives, and we all run into challenges like T.J.'s altitude sickness. Perhaps it's a simple challenge, or maybe it's something that threatens your entire existence. The Everest Model is the way to navigate those challenges. Once you have built a Foundation, and strengthened your Core, your Behaviour will pull you through any situation with your team by your side.

My boardroom experience at some organizations saw some pretty shady characters. It's a fact of life – it is hard not to get sucked into the negativism that sometimes pervades our work environment. But following the ingredients inside the Behaviour Principle will greatly increase your odds of success.

Now let's look at it from another angle. Who do you want around you when you are hiking up that mountain? I know that I want people like T.J. around: individuals who have the strength and perseverance to continue even when they are presented with seemingly insurmountable challenges.

The people I was lucky to have around me during my time at Bain Capital were people who were true masters of Behaviour – individuals who, like my son on Everest, look towards the Mission with the help of Community. These are also the people who display a positive attitude as they're trekking along the trail.

How would you come in to work when times are tough? Imagine this:

- There are cash flow issues.

- There are competitive issues.

- There are personnel issues.

- A natural disaster comes through.

- Your supplier goes out of business.

- Someone sues you.

All of these things are challenges that every business faces on a day-to-day basis and all kinds of leaders, both great and small, are tasked with the responsibility of overcoming.

If you come in every day and give the "woe is me" speech to your team, and you lack Resolve, Virtue and Focus, you will have a hard time having anyone on your team display Resolve, Virtue and Focus. Model the Behaviour you want to see in your team, and you will be amazed to see that it works.

T.J. and I knew what we had to do during our trek on Mount Everest, and we had to achieve it with Resolve, Virtue and Focus. That's no different than my Bain Capital experience, where we had a clear Mission and a team with a strong sense of Community. And my experience at Bain was no different than any one of the successful experiences I had in my 25 years in various boardrooms. Each one of those experiences had challenges, difficult people and disruptions, but it always went right when we made a conscious choice to be surrounded by the right Behaviours. With people alongside me who displayed Resolve, Virtue and Focus, we were able to climb straight to the top.

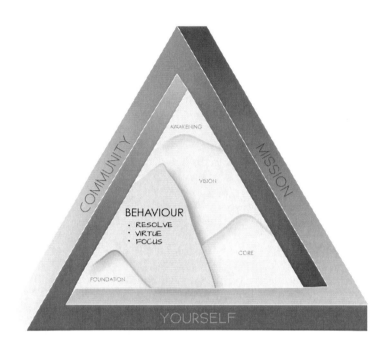

BEHAVIOUR
Ingredient #1: Resolve

- Your behaviour defines your commitment to resolve.

- Resolve can be lonely. But it's important.

- Leadership demands the confidence found in solid resolve.

- Resolve is freedom from indecision. Make strong decisions that are based on your Foundation and Core.

APPLICATIONS – *RESOLVE*

1. List times that you have displayed Resolve:

At home   *At work*

_____   _____

_____   _____

_____   _____

2. What is difficult for you about acting with resolve? Why?

_____

_____

3. When have you been indecisive?

At Home   *At Work*

_____   _____

_____   _____

_____   _____

4. What damage did your indecision cause? What could you do to have less indecision in your life?

_____

_____

BEHAVIOUR
Ingredient #2: Virtue

- Lead with virtue, and everyone will follow.
- Stand your ground!
- Do what is right and avoid doing what is wrong.
- Place what is right above all else.
- Be honorable, good, admirable and honest.
- Act and communicate with virtue even when it is painful.
- Giving up and giving in are not always the best solution to conflict. Hang on to your true self and demonstrate it without resorting to aggression.

APPLICATIONS – *VIRTUE*

1. List a few people and businesses that have great Virtue:

    Companies   *People*

    _____   _____

    _____   _____

    _____   _____

2. How do those people and companies do "what's right"?

_____

_____

3. When have you given up or given in?

    At Home   *At Work*

    _____   _____

    _____   _____

    _____   _____

4. How could you better *not* give up, but also *not* resort to aggressive Behaviour?

_____

_____

BEHAVIOUR
Ingredient #3: Focus

- Focus requires great discipline.
- Focus leads to results.
- Try to eliminate distractions and focus on your goal or objective.
- Here are four checks to keeping your focus:
    1. Act and speak with dignity
    2. Follow the 80/20 rule. (80% of the time, you should be listening.)
    3. Identify first, then react.
    4. Acknowledge that there is a power at work that is bigger than you.

APPLICATIONS – *FOCUS*

1. Where and at what times do you have the best focus?

       At home   *At work*

       _____   _____

       _____   _____

       _____   _____

2. What could you do to channel that focus better?

_____

_____

3. What are some major distractions for you?

       At Home   *At Work*

       _____   _____

       _____   _____

       _____   _____

4. How can you build your discipline and focus?

_____

_____

Everyone's eyes are on you. If you are leading a group of trekkers up the mountain, you want them to watch you and be inspired. This is no different than when you are leading or managing a group of individuals in the workplace. Your actions will inspire your teammates, and they will aspire to duplicate your successful Behaviour. Here are three things to remember for the journey:

1. You will be judged by your actions.

2. Your actions are very loud!

3. You only have control over how you react.

We can all build a stable Foundation, strengthen our Core, and then work to have the right Behaviours for success. And when we do these first three principles, we will see incredible results in every corner of our lives.

There are only two remaining principles after these, but they are equally important: Vision and Awakening. Just as the final mile of our trip to Mount Everest Base Camp was the most difficult, these last two principles are in many ways the most difficult. But they will be worth the effort!

APPLICATIONS – *BEHAVIOUR*

1. What did your parents and teachers say about your Behaviour as a child? Is that how you still operate today?

_____

_____

2. How can a few adjustments in your Behaviour help to positively influence your personal and business life?

_____

_____

3. List things you could do to adjust your Behaviour.

Personal Life	*Professional Life*
_____	_____
_____	_____
_____	_____

4. What are a few thoughts about the person you would most like to be, both at home and at work? What steps can you take to get there?

_____

_____

EVEREST MODEL
Principle Four: Vision

*"Vision is the art of seeing
what is invisible to others."*
- Jonathan Swift

Vision is a word we hear all the time in a corporate context, but we rarely stop to think about what it actually means. Let's think about it in terms of Mount Everest.

One of the most interesting aspects of the trek to Base Camp is that there are only a few times that you can actually see the summit of Mount Everest. And even then, the conditions have to be perfect to catch a glimpse of the world's tallest peak. In fact, as you get closer to Base Camp, although you would think you might be able to see the peak more easily, you couldn't see the peak at all.

Symbolically these two situations are very similar to our personal and professional lives. Many times we are working towards the Vision, but we can't actually *see* it with clarity. And other times, we can clearly see the Vision, but we are still far away from it.

There was a moment when T.J. and I were trekking back down from Mount Everest Base Camp – leaving the town of Lobuche – when we arrived at an incredible ridge, known as Memorial Hill. (As a side note, this felt like much more than a "hill" – in Canada, we would call it a "ridge".) Memorial Hill is a very special place – sacred, in fact. On top, there are monuments and tombstones for all the trekkers who have perished in their pursuit of summiting Everest.

We arrived and the wind was blowing strong across the ridge. Colorful prayer flags were draped all across the tombstones, and they were blowing in the cold breeze. You couldn't help but remain quiet, taking a moment to reflect on your life, and on your journey.

As we looked off the edge of Memorial Hill, we saw the most magnificent, vast valley below us. I asked Byron Smith (our guide and a Canadian trekker who had summited Everest and the six other highest peaks in the world) which direction we were headed. He pointed off in the distance towards the small village of Pheriche. From here, I could clearly see the next day's journey. It was a magnificent sight.

Just like at that moment atop Memorial Hill, many times in business we can see our destination in front of us, and we clearly see the path to get there. That was the situation during my time at Bain Capital. We all knew what we needed to do, and where we needed to go. Unfortunately, that didn't make getting there any easier, but it made the journey a magnificent one.

Other times, even though our Vision may not be in sight – as it so clearly was for me at Bain, and with T.J. on top of Memorial Hill – we need to be able to clearly articulate and describe that Vision. On the way up to Base Camp, T.J. and I weren't able to see our destination until we were a mile away.

We understood ultimately what our goal was, and we strove towards that particular goal. It sounds simple, but it was incredibly difficult.

There are many organizations that put up flowery vision statements, and others that are more minimalist in their approaches. That doesn't matter as much: whatever approach keeps you focused on the goal is fine. The most important thing is that it be a *strong* Vision.

In the case of our Base Camp experience, the Vision was pretty clear. We were venturing off on a journey that was in a far away land, starting our trek in Lukla and traveling up a mountain to the destination of Mount Everest Base Camp, just under 19,000 feet.

In order to work towards achieving our vision in this case, we had to align our values with the Vision. This is very important, whether in our home or business lives. We need to really adopt the Vision as our own, and work hard to make it happen.

T.J. and I quickly figured out that this trip to Everest was going to be an adventure of a lifetime. Therefore, *adventurousness* was a value that T.J. and I had to wholeheartedly embrace – and we did.

Next, it was easy to align with the Sir Edmund Hillary Foundation's purpose for the trip – helping people in a far-off land to build schools and medical centers. That lined right up with our family's values.

Long story short, T.J. and I were really able to adopt this Vision, even though the whole adventure had started when I raised my hand after a couple of glasses of wine. I didn't have a New Year's Resolution in 2010 to purchase a trip to Mount Everest Base Camp. But once I bought the trip, we aligned our values with the trip's Vision, and it became our own.

There are many times in life when we find ourselves in various circumstances when we start questioning, "Is this venture or project something that we should do or not?" In the case of Base Camp, or any other experience in life, once you find yourself in a certain circumstance, working for a particular company, undertaking a volunteer endeavour, or in a community program, you have to figure out whether or not your Values align with that program or company.

When we have a well-rooted value structure around our Vision, that Vision becomes much more achievable. I felt this in planning our Base Camp trip, and I felt it in the boardroom throughout my career in business. Once you have established that connection between your personal and your family's values, you are not going to give up. You're not going to walk away from your *own* Vision.

That said, there were certainly times that I was questioning our Vision in various boardrooms and certainly on the trek to Base Camp. That is almost a given when you take on a challenging goal. More than a few times (especially while in the middle of challenging climbs) I thought to myself, "What the heck am I doing up here on the tallest peak in the world?" But there was always another voice in my head that reminded me about the greater Vision.

I have worked for, and with, many leaders who have struggled to reach their Vision. In nearly every case, that Vision wasn't shared and *owned* by everyone on the team, it was poorly communicated, and there were no mentors reinforcing the direction.

Vision is never achieved alone. As a leader in business or in your personal life, you need to follow the critical ingredients. Surround yourself with mentors who will assist and guide you towards the Vision, choose carefully the steps towards the Vision and behave with solid leadership. It is not good enough to simply post the Vision on the walls. You need to live it out.

As was the case in the trek to Base Camp, we understood the Vision, we were prepared to mentor each other, we made informed choices as to what we were getting into, and we had great leadership.

Look for those three ingredients as you develop your own vision (and most certainly before getting on a plane to Nepal).

After establishing a Vision that we can align with our root values, we need to go through the process of reaching our destination. As I mentioned earlier, this is not as easy as it seems. The three key ingredients of Vision in the Everest Model will ultimately help you to reach your destination. Those ingredients are Mentorship, Choice and Leadership.

1. Sometimes you lead, and sometimes you follow. In fact, the greatest leaders always know when it is appropriate to follow others. This is called Mentorship, and is as old as civilization. It's incredibly important in the interest of successfully executing on a Vision.

Throughout our lives, whether in school, at home, or at work, sometimes we are mentoring and other times we are being mentored. That has certainly been the case in my career. A large part of the work I now do would fall under the category of mentoring others – and certainly, during my time in the boardroom, I spent a great deal of time mentoring members of my team. Nevertheless, as I advanced in my career, I began to realize that there are certain times when it's much better to sit down, shut up and listen. Of course, this is also a lesson we all need to learn in order to be a good partner to our spouse, a good parent to our kids, and a good friend.

Mentorship is all about listening – not just doing all of the talking. Some of my greatest mentors, in fact, have listened to me more than they have talked. In fact, if you find yourself in any situation doing all of the talking, there might be something wrong!

Surround yourself with the right individuals, and whether you are a mentor, a mentee or both, realize that you cannot do this alone.

>   2. All of your Choices will have consequences. Any Choice is okay as long as you are prepared to accept the consequences of that Choice.

Every day I tell my corporate clients, "There is a lot of power in Choice." We have the power to choose just about anything. Every single day, we make choice after choice. If you have ever seen a two-year old, they are already making Choices – and from then on, we create our own road map.

What actions do I want to take? What's the most important thing to me over the next hour? What task am I going to be accomplishing today?

When you have a chance to join an organization, are you joining it because the work fits your competency? Are you there because your salary meets your expectations and there are career growth opportunities? Before you accept the job, ask yourself the question, "Will I be accepted in this environment?" Think about whether you will be able to balance work and home life in a way that makes you feel comfortable and fulfilled. Do you hold common root values with the rest of the team members?

A simple example of this would be: if you're a person who is very environmentally conscious, are you joining an organization that doesn't even think about the environment when it comes to their day-to-day business? If so, that would not be a good alignment in terms of your values and their Vision.

3. Finally, in the case of Leadership – when you are leading your organization – make sure that, after you have defined your core values, after you have articulated your Vision to everyone on the team, be steadfast. Make sure that you continue to strive towards that Vision. That is true Leadership.

I have seen inside many organizations where the Vision is lofty, but it's just not communicated well enough (as a result of some inadequacies in leadership). Those organizations have a very hard time reaching that Vision.

If you are the leader, are you displaying the qualities of your Vision on a regular basis? Have you set out a solid Vision, in terms of what direction you're heading? Are you clear in your articulation of the Vision?

On the flip side, if you are an individual who is part of an organization or trekking up a mountain, are you comfortable with your leadership? Are you comfortable with the direction that you're heading?

Come up with a courageous and inspiring Vision for your team – not one that is necessarily flowery in its wording, but something that can truly make a difference, within your life and within the lives of others. Aim for your own Everest – you'll get there, step by step.

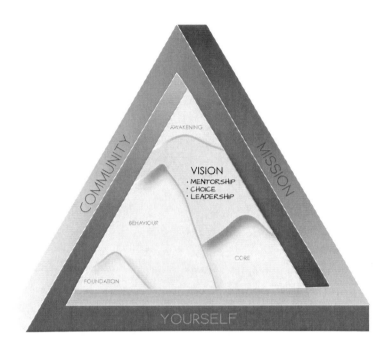

VISION
Ingredient #1: Mentorship

- Mentors don't *do*. They *coach* and *advise*.
- Learning is a continual process, and it happens via mentors.
- Your success will come from the confidence you attain when you are a strong mentor to others.
- You don't have to be lonely as a leader.
- Work hard to be a trusted guide and advisor.

APPLICATIONS – *MENTORSHIP*

1. List a few of your Mentors and your Mentees:

      Mentors   *Mentees*

      _____   _____

      _____   _____

      _____   _____

2. What are your strengths and weaknesses as a Mentor?

_____

_____

3. When have you learned the most from others recently?

      At Home   *At Work*

      _____   _____

      _____   _____

      _____   _____

4. How could you be a better Mentor? What can you do to learn more from others?

_____

_____

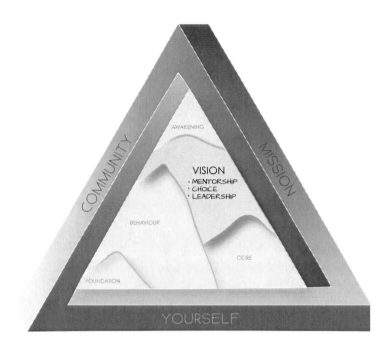

VISION
Ingredient #2: Choice

- True power lies in choice.

- Everything you do starts with a choice. Are you prepared to accept the consequences?

- What is most important to you in any given situation? Follow that question up by asking yourself, "Really?"

- Are you a slave to the choices you have made? Don't forget that you always have another choice!

- Intuitions are our best counselors. Follow them.

APPLICATIONS – *CHOICE*

1. List a few choices you have every day:

   At Home   *At Work*

   _____   _____

   _____   _____

   _____   _____

2. Have you ever been a "slave" to a choice you've made?

   _____

   _____

3. How can you better follow your intuitions?

   At Home   *At Work*

   _____   _____

   _____   _____

   _____   _____

4. What are a few ways that choices will give you strength?

   _____

   _____

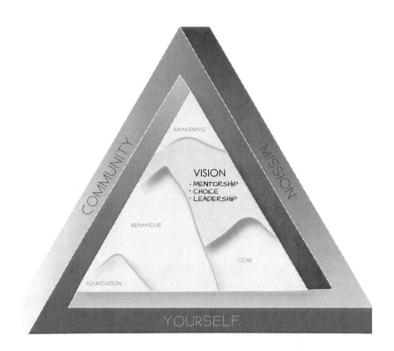

VISION
Ingredient #3: Leadership

- A leader must be able to mobilize, focus, inspire and rejuvenate those they lead.
- Do you have the capacity to influence and inspire others in order to fulfill your team's common Vision?
- Sometimes you will lead, and other times, you must follow. Take time to be a mentee as well as a mentor from time to time.

APPLICATIONS – *LEADERSHIP*

1. How do you lead, and how do you follow?

       Leading   *Following*

_____

_____

_____

2. What are some of the ways you could be a better leader?

_____

_____

3. How have you inspired, mobilized or rejuvenated people?

       At Home   *At Work*

_____

_____

_____

4. How can you better influence others in order to inspire them to aim for your common Vision?

_____

_____

If you are on the shoulder of Mount Everest, and you don't have a map of where you are headed, you are going to get lost or worse – very quickly. The same applies for every other aspect of our lives. We need that map, or Vision.

Rethink what it means to write a Vision Statement – this is not just a pretty paragraph that will make your investors or your mother happy. The Vision is a map to the peak of Mount Everest. It's a map to the destination that you can reach if you put all of your effort towards it.

- Commit to your new Vision Statement.

- Take action to make this Vision Statement come true. Use it in everything you do.

- As the Vision provides your destination – the "where you want to get to" – all of your goals and strategies will focus on making it happen. It is the basis for all of your actions. Clarity of *direction* comes from well-sighted Vision.

- Keep your Vision alive. Share it with everyone. If you just tell your Vision to people once, your vision will fade and disappear. Talk about it, and keep your vision alive by keeping it prominent in your office, so that all will be reminded of it daily.

- Dare to dream! However, before you can travel to the moon, you have to look up at the stars. You can't get to your destination until you know which direction you are heading!

- In order to establish a great Vision, focus back on the basics. Where are you going to be five years from now? What will you have accomplished?

As you trek the journey towards your Vision, you'll again find that you understand your own values better than you ever have. You will connect with your Community, and together articulate and achieve your Mission.

We are near the peak of the Everest Model, and as the air grows thin near the top, we will proceed towards Awakening, the final principle.

APPLICATIONS – *VISION*

1. Shape your Vision Statement here – or reshape it if you already have one.

_____

_____

2. Where will you be three years from now?

_____

_____

3. What are some Visions you have in your life?

Personal Life	*Professional Life*
_____	_____
_____	_____
_____	_____

4. Do your core values align with the Visions you have listed above? How do you communicate these as a leader?

_____

_____

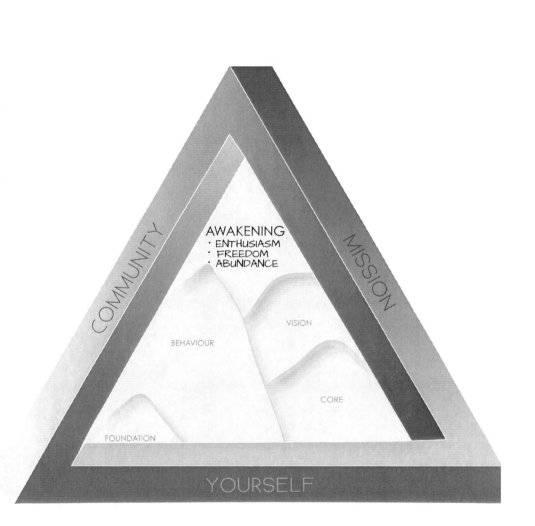

EVEREST MODEL

Principle Five: *Awakening*

"If every day is an awakening, you will never grow old. You will just keep growing."
- Gail Sheehy

Awakening is what we all strive to achieve. It's beyond Vision. It's the realization of the Vision. It's the achievement. And with that achievement we embrace Enthusiasm, we have a sense of Freedom, and are filled with Abundance.

This is the ultimate success that we have strived towards for so long. My son and I reached Base Camp of Mount Everest and had our picture taken together. Bain Capital sold SuperPages Canada for a profit of $700 million dollars.

This is that moment when all of your efforts, and all of the fruits of your labor pay off. You score big for the home team, and now it's time to do a dance in the end zone. You are finally at the moment in the Everest Model that I call Awakening.

Many people have asked me about my Base Camp experience, or my Bain Capital experience. Once we have had a conversation about one or both events in my life, some say, "That must have been life-altering!" I don't look at it that way at all. They were both incredible moments in time. Indeed, when I think back about what resonated most with me during T.J. and my trek on Mount Everest, there were many things that I will never forget, but I don't think those things were life-altering. They were Awakening moments.

Traveling through the Himalayan Mountains, we had a chance to see many little villages, where our guides from the Sir Edmund Hillary Foundation brought us to the schools and medical clinics they had built. T.J. and I realized the impact that one individual can have on a great many people's lives. We saw how these schools and clinics truly made the Sherpa people's lives better – we saw their jubilation and excitement over their improved and still improving lives. This was an Awakening experience for me, but it still was not life-altering. If anything, it cemented the principles that I hold most dear.

Upon arriving at Khumjung and attending the 50th anniversary of the Sir Edmond Hillary School, T.J. and I were given the opportunity to present a check to the headmaster for $5,000 dollars. This was a wonderful experience that was part of our Awakening moment.

Prior to our departure to Nepal, we decided to see if we could raise some additional funds to support and celebrate the anniversary. We had postcards of a mountain scene in Canada produced, and for a minimum donation of $1 dollar, we sold postcards to our community. People would write a message, and then give them back to us to bring to the Himalayan Mountains with us on our journey.

On the day of the anniversary in Khumjung, I had the honor of reading a few cards from children in Canada to the Sherpa Children of the Khumjung School. We left the postcards as a keepsake for all of the children there. This was a brief moment in our lives that had a big impact on us, and on the schoolchildren in two countries across the globe from one another.

At the moment of an Awakening, we ask ourselves, "What is really important in my life?" This happens when we achieve our Vision, and this is our moment of reflection. It is our time to sit back and say, "Well, what does this particular achievement mean to me?" This Awakening moment becomes a validation of the values that supported you towards that Vision.

We were in Khumjung for a few nights before preparing for our final departure back to Kathmandu. The 50th anniversary celebration going on all around us was wonderfully symbolic of our Awakening – and was certainly the climax of our journey. I vividly remember our last evening there, at a student party, outdoors for the entire village to enjoy.

I watched as high school students laughed and danced outdoors with music and lights. I couldn't help but whisper under my breath, "It's never enough," as I looked at all of these kids having an amazing time with so little. Those words that the Boston businessman had told me years before couldn't have been more distant from the truth. These children were living examples of "it's enough." Awakening is not tied to the notion that you have to *have* more. It is tied to your Vision, and whether you reach that Vision.

Just as on our Base Camp journey, we weren't home yet, Awakening is not the last step in business or in life, and that's what I like most about the Everest Model. When you climb a mountain, you go up to your destination. Then at some point, you come back down. Most mountain climbers choose to then find another mountain, climb it, and so on, with mountain after mountain until they retire. That's what our lives are like – a series of mountains that we summit and descend from. This is a cycle, not a linear path, and when you have achieved Awakening, you will cycle back around again to the very beginning, where you build another Foundation, strengthen your Core, work on your Behaviour, create a Vision, and reach Awakening yet again.

The most important aspect of Awakening is the process of learning. Next time you can do things a little bit better. You can learn from each step you took on this particular journey – and the next will be easier, smoother, and potentially even more successful.

Now think back to what it was like to be a small child. We cycled through the stages of the Everest Model extremely quickly – learning, awakening and changing. This is a process that we are very familiar with, and that we can use to significantly improve our lives. Awakening has the ingredients of Enthusiasm, Freedom and Abundance.

1. It's okay to take time to celebrate! It's okay to reflect on your successes with Enthusiasm. Just don't let it go to your head! Don't get too hung up on yourself: you're not bigger than life, no matter what success you've enjoyed, large or small.

You put your pants on the same way as everybody else! Take time to acknowledge others who participated in this success. Allow yourself to experience the Enthusiasm, and have a moment of reflection and recognition, but then move on.

2. The most incredible thing I felt while we were trekking on Mount Everest was Freedom. Freedom can be incredibly powerful within a corporation, but it can also be very damaging. When you stand on a cliff, enjoy the view, but be careful not to take a step too close to the edge!

Don't just feel the exhilaration and Enthusiasm of achieving your Vision. Also use this moment to take better care of yourself – to think back to the earlier ingredient Balance, and feel the freedom of good health and enough rest. Take time to be with your family and friends, and to enjoy life – that is the truest freedom there is.

This is also a time when you can feel free to tell the truth, and to evaluate how far you've come. While we were still starting our trip up Mount Everest, I was walking just behind T.J. and Byron, when I heard Byron ask my 16-year old son, "So, T.J., tell me one thing that you have learned so far!"

T.J. responded to the veteran trekker without missing a beat. He said, enthusiastically, "Value everything you have."

I thought that was really profound for a teenaged boy to say. He really realized how thankful we should be for all of the things we have at our fingertips in our North American home environment.

Take advantage of the days you can spend in this Awakening stage. Have as many conversations as you can, ask questions, listen for answers, and enjoy the celebration.

3. I cycle back now to what the Boston businessman said to me after the huge business deal that made Bain Capital $700 million dollars. He told me, "It will never be enough." Think about that statement in your own life when you are at the Awakening stage. Carefully consider your choice, and then do what you feel is best for Yourself, your Community, and your Mission.

Our trip to Nepal taught both T.J. and me that we had Abundance in our lives at home that people around the world simply cannot share. We already had more than enough.

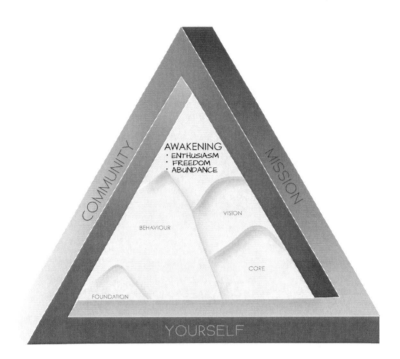

AWAKENING
Ingredient #1: Enthusiasm

- It is always better to help others be successful and know you had a part in that.

- Don't let yourself become too attached to the celebration. Allow others to feel it first.

- Allow yourself a feeling of extreme joy when things go right. It's all right to celebrate!

APPLICATIONS – *ENTHUSIASM*

1. Who made this success possible? List a few names here.

_____   _____

_____   _____

_____   _____

2. Are there ways that you can thank those people in an unexpected and special way?

_____

_____

3. Describe a few situations of pure celebration:

At Home   *At Work*

_____   _____

_____   _____

_____   _____

4. What can you learn from this? Where do you go next?

_____

_____

_____

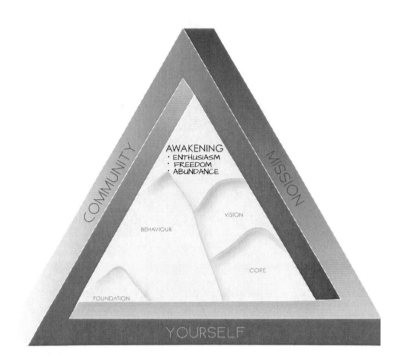

AWAKENING
Ingredient #2: Freedom

- Don't get too attached to anything.

- You are not in control! There is a higher power at work.

- Look after yourself – feel the freedom of good health and enough rest.

- Tell the truth.

- Always show up and be present, but feel free to express yourself and be honest to your mission.

APPLICATIONS – *FREEDOM*

1. List some things that you might be too attached to:

_____   _____

_____   _____

_____   _____

2. How can you work towards the freedom of good health?

_____

_____

3. When have you expressed yourself most honestly:

At Home   *At Work*

_____   _____

_____   _____

_____   _____

4. What are some ways that you can bring a sense of freedom to everyone around you?

_____

_____

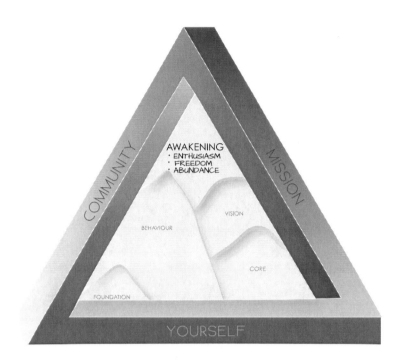

AWAKENING
Ingredient #3: Abundance

- A larger-than-adequate supply does not mean you have a surplus.
- Is it ever enough?
- Stay focused on what is important.
- Set realistic personal and professional goals.
- Give without request for return, and you will achieve Abundance.

APPLICATIONS – *ABUNDANCE*

1. What is most important to you?

At Home   *At Work*

_____   _____

_____   _____

_____   _____

2. What are a few realistic personal & professional goals?

_____

_____

3. What are a few ways you could give a little more to others, without asking for anything in return?

At Home   *At Work*

_____   _____

_____   _____

_____   _____

4. What does Abundance mean to you?

_____

_____

Everyone asks themselves the question from time to time, "Is bigger better?" Are we really happier with an over-abundance of clutter in our lives? Do we need a big house, a big car, and a big screen television over the fireplace? The answer for many of us is, "it's never enough," and we have a hard time seeing ourselves as living in a land of Abundance.

As I think about my Awakening moments, and I think about the Abundance ingredient in all of this, *more* is not necessarily *better*. Let's not live in the disposable society I mentioned earlier in the book, where relationships and friendships can be thrown away along with last year's electronics.

Awakening is the time when you have a chance to look at everything with fresh eyes, and it is *so* important to take a pause to reflect on the whirlwind that just happened. I can't imagine what I would have done if I hadn't taken time to think about my Bain Capital experience, spending time with my family and feeling the Freedom of thought that comes to us when we are at the summit of the Everest Model.

When we are standing on top of a mountain, we take time to look around. Do the same in your own life – it will make a big difference. Now is the time.

APPLICATIONS – *AWAKENING*

1. Describe an Awakening moment you have had.

_____

_____

2. How did you celebrate that Awakening moment?

_____

_____

3. What are the most valuable things in your life?

Personal Life	*Professional Life*
_____	_____
_____	_____
_____	_____

4. If you look around your life as if it were a mountain vista, what do you see?

_____

_____

"You've climbed the highest mountain in the world. What's left? It's all downhill from there. You've got to set your sights on something higher than Everest."

- Willi Unsoeld

Conclusion

At the tail end of our trip on Mount Everest, as T.J. and I and the other trekkers started coming down from Base Camp, we slowly descended back towards our day-to-day lives. All signs of T.J.'s altitude sickness had gone away, and we sensed that our adventure was nearing its end. But there were still a few things left in store.

At the tail end of the trip, we were on route to Khumjung Village, where Sir Edmund Hillary had decided that he was going to build the most pronounced district for schools in the area. Over the years, his organization built several schools there, from high schools on down to grade schools, and a medical center in Kunde.

We were very excited, because we had been invited to participate in the 50th Anniversary of the first school that Sir Edmund Hillary started with Zeke

O'Connor. In addition to all of that and unbeknownst to me at the time, we also would be visiting Monument Hill, where the Sherpa people of Khumjung Valley had built a monument to commemorate the life of Sir Edmund Hillary, his wife and his daughter.

The tragic story of Sir Edmund Hillary's wife and daughter is that they died in a plane crash in the Himalayan Mountains on one of their many visits to the region. The Sherpa people built the monuments to commemorate both women, and eventually Sir Edmund himself, when he died in 2008. To the north, you could see the trail to Base Camp of Everest. And although you couldn't see Base Camp, you could see the peak of Everest from part of the hill.

From each corner of the hill, you could stand and look out over different parts of the valley – different streams flowing in every direction. You could see for miles and miles. It was an unbelievable view - absolutely spectacular.

As T.J. and I stood before this monument at the top of this tall hill, we realized in wonder how vast the Himalayan Mountains were, and how many little villages stretched out below our feet. It was almost as if Sir Edmund Hillary was given a monument here where he would be able to see how the people he cared so much about were faring.

We were experiencing another Awakening moment, as we were reminded of how simple and tremendous life can be, relative to what you contribute to the wellbeing of others. Many children have been impacted by the schools built by the Sir Edmund Hillary Foundation, and many lives have been saved with the medicine at the Khunde Hillary Hospital.

When I think back on that experience, I can't help but remember my time in boardrooms. So many of them were so focused on things that were specific to greed and the bottom line. Of course I understand the importance of money to philanthropic causes, but there is still a huge dichotomy there.

My friend David Howe says it best, "It's all about making a difference while making a dollar." If more and more boardrooms could embrace that kind of thinking, the world would truly change for the better – and quickly.

I truly loved my time working for Bain Capital, and I experienced one of the highest highs in my life during that seven-month period. We were responsible for one of the biggest profits Bain has ever enjoyed in one transaction. I could never forget how we joyfully clinked our glasses of champagne together and toasted to our overwhelming success. But I will also never forget that Boston businessman who came up to me and said, "Remember, Todd, it is never enough."

Six years later, I stood at the top of Monument Hill in Nepal next to my son, and we clinked our water bottles together, toasting a successful journey through the Himalayan Mountains. We had spent 30 days seeing things that most people will never see – sharing an incredible adventure together as father and son. We sipped out of our bottles of water as we looked at the monument to Sir Edmund Hillary and contemplated his great impact on the world.

I knew at that moment that it was enough.

About the Author

Todd Millar was formally involved with one of the most successful Private Equity transactions in the history of Bain Capital – the acquisition of SuperPages Canada for $1.9 billion dollars, and less than a year later, its sale for $2.6 billion dollars. After 25 years in senior executive positions in the petroleum, telecommunications, and advertising industries, Millar is now a national speaker and executive coach, as well as immediate Past-President of the world's largest hockey association, Hockey Calgary. He has been involved in a number of volunteer organizations, including various hockey organizations, the Juvenile Diabetes Research Foundation, the Calgary Stampede and the National Adoption Association.

If you can't find Millar on the ice officiating a hockey game, he might be scuba diving, climbing to Base Camp of Everest or zip lining across a rain forest.

Find out more at *www.toddmillarspeaking.com*

The Sir Edmund Hillary Foundation

The author will be donating a portion of the proceeds of the sales of this book to The Sir Edmund Hillary Foundation. Here are a few words about the organization.

Zeke O'Connor first visited Nepal in April 1973, as the Canadian representative and guest of Sir Edmund Hillary and the 1953 British Everest Team visiting Nepal on the 20th Anniversary of their conquest of Mount Everest. Their commemorative trek was to the Mount Everest Base Camp area. One year later, O'Connor founded The Sir Edmund Hillary Foundation in Canada, in order to assist Sir Edmund Hillary with his work benefitting the Sherpa people of the Solu Khumbu area in Nepal.

During O'Connor's four decades as Founder-President, the organization has raised millions of dollars for Nepal to build schools, hospitals, medical clinics, provide medical scholarships, train village health workers, install water pipelines, build bridges and trekking paths during flash floods, and to fully fund the Kunde Hospital and Sagarmatha National

Park reforestation programs. The Foundation has worked closely with the National Park Department in Kathmandu, and to this date, more than 1.5 million seedlings have been planted in Sagarmatha National Park.

O'Connor visits Nepal each year with a number of the Foundation's Directors, and each time they return to Canada, they have a deeper understanding of the many needs of the Sherpa people. They also have a strong determination to seek financial aid for the worthy projects underway in the mountain regions of Nepal, emphasizing the involvement of the local community. As part of that initiative, the Board of Directors of The Sir Edmund Hillary Foundation has recently approved a project to revitalize the Sherpa language in this region.

The proceeds of this book will help the Sir Edmund Hillary Foundation continue to improve the quality of life for the Sherpa people, staying steadfast in its commitments to health, education and the environment of the Solu Khumbu area in Nepal.

For more information, please visit the organization's website: *www.thesiredmundhillaryfoundation.ca*